PLATO
The Last Days of Socrates

*

EUTHYPHRO

THE APOLOGY

CRITO

PHAEDO

*

Translated and with an Introduction by
HUGH TREDENNICK

PENGUIN BOOKS
BALTIMORE · MARYLAND

Penguin Books Ltd, Harmondsworth, Middlesex
U.S.A.: Penguin Books Inc., 3300 Clipper Mill Road, Baltimore 11, Md
AUSTRALIA: Penguin Books Pty Ltd, 762 Whitehorse Road,
Mitcham, Victoria

—

Published in Penguin Books 1954
Reprinted 1955, 1957, 1958
New edition, with additions, 1959
Reprinted 1961

Made and printed in Great Britain
by The Whitefriars Press Ltd,
London and Tonbridge

CONTENTS

INTRODUCTION

THE fifth century before Christ was a period of extraordinary activity and achievement in the Greek world. A new spirit of enterprise, inspired by the defeat of the great Persian invasion, led to rapid development and expansion in every department of life. This spirit had its focus in Athens, where, under the guidance of Pericles, political and commercial prosperity was crowned with the most perfect flowers of art and literature; but everywhere men's minds were restlessly experimenting and reaching out for knowledge. By the middle of the century science and philosophy – still indistinguishable and less than 150 years old – had made considerable progress, especially in the direction of physics. Lacking instruments of precision, such as the microscope, Greek thinkers could only proceed by simple observation and reasoning; yet they were already close to a reasonable atomic theory. But the mass of experience and collected information was not co-ordinated, and speculation followed different lines in different schools of thought, which had little in common except confidence in their own doctrines and a hearty contempt for the theories of others. The conflict of voices was stimulating but extremely confusing, and the ordinary man really did not know whom or what to believe.

In this intellectual ferment there arose a new class of people called Sophists or Wise Men. They were not – at least not essentially – philosophers or scientists, but professional itinerant teachers. Many were really able and had something positive and valuable to impart; but others encouraged scepticism by stressing the two-sidedness of every question, or undermined faith in real values by preaching a kind of subjectivism or relativism. On the whole their outlook was at once superficial and practical; they said in effect 'Knowledge is impossible, but I can show you how to make the most of yourself'. So they aimed at producing cleverness and efficiency rather than wisdom and goodness; and they charged fees for their services – which shocked the philosophers, but was good psychology as well as good business, since people take seriously what they have to pay for. In short, the old religious and moral ideals were giving way to a creed of materialistic opportunism. The voice of a prophet was badly needed.

*

Socrates was born at Athens in the year 469 B.C. His father was a sculptor and his mother had been a midwife. It is not clear whether he had any profession of his own, but the fact that during middle life he served in the army as a self-equipped 'hoplite' or heavy-armed infantryman shows that he had some means then, even if he was later reduced to poverty. He must have been quite fifty when he married Xanthippe (perhaps his second wife), whose reputation as a shrew lacks reliable evidence.

We know much more about the man himself than about his career. Portraits and descriptions make it plain that he had a heavy, rather ugly face, with a snub nose, prominent eyes beneath shaggy eyebrows, and a large full mouth. He was bearded and (in his later years at any rate) bald. His thickset body had great strength and extraordinary powers of endurance. He strutted as he walked, always went barefoot, and would often stand in a trance for hours. These external oddities made him a cartoonist's dream, and it is not surprising that Aristophanes caricatured him in the *Clouds*. On the other hand his mind, though not creative, was exceptionally clear, critical and eager. It tolerated no pretence; and since his will was as strong as his convictions, his conduct was as logical as his thinking. In a sceptical age he believed firmly in moral goodness as the one thing that matters; and he identified it with knowledge, because to his straightforward nature it seemed inconceivable that anyone should see what is right without doing it. This simple view has excited more contempt than it deserves, since there would not be much wrong with it if we all had his honesty and self-control.

But he was not merely a moralist; he was a sincerely religious man. So much is certain, although it is not possible to say exactly what he believed. The fact that Plato (or his translator) often makes him speak of 'God' or 'the god' proves nothing, because these were common forms of speech; besides, Plato himself was certainly feeling his way towards monotheism. Nevertheless it is quite possible that Socrates, though accepting orthodox beliefs and performing the traditional rites, regarded the various gods less as separate beings than as different aspects of a single Godhead. His belief in a supernatural voice which deterred him from wrong courses of action points in this direction; for it makes no difference whether the 'sign' was an illusion or the voice of conscience or a rare mystical experience – he believed in it and apparently did not attribute it to any particular deity.*

With all these qualities Socrates might easily have been a combination of pedant, prig, and fanatic. In fact, his kindly heart, his quick perception, his unfailing tact and patience and cheerfulness – all enlivened by an impish sense of humour – made him an ideal companion; and although he offended many people who did not like having their shams and shoddy ways of thinking exposed, all honest seekers of the truth admired and revered him, while by his closer friends he was loved with utter devotion.

It is important to emphasize Socrates' humanity, because he still affects people's minds in widely different ways. To some, who prefer a Launcelot to a Galahad, or who feel uneasy before those steady eyes, his rectitude seems quite inhuman – an intolerable superiority. Others, naturally inclined to hero-worship and impressed by features in his character and story, try to raise him to forbidden heights by comparing him with the Man who was also God. Socrates was not even a martyr – that is, not in the Christian sense. He was a prophet, but no more.

*

How Socrates' mind developed we can only guess. He was associated for some time with the Athenian philosopher Archelaus, and it was almost certainly through Archelaus that he became acquainted (as we are told in the *Phaedo*) with the doctrines of Anaxagoras. He must have met and talked with most of the great thinkers of his day, because they nearly all visited Athens, and he never missed the chance of debating with an expert. He showed up so well in these encounters that (according to the story quoted in the *Apology*) one of his friends ventured to ask the oracle at Delphi whether anyone was wiser than Socrates, and received the answer No.

However we are to take this story, there is little doubt that Socrates believed it and was at first genuinely perturbed, until it dawned upon him that his wisdom lay in recognition of his

---

* When he speaks of himself as a servant of Apollo he is thinking of the 'mission' laid upon him by the Apolline oracle at Delphi (pp. 49–50).

own ignorance; and that it was the oracle's intention that he should convince others of their ignorance too, and so help them on the way to knowledge and goodness. From this time onwards his interest was concentrated upon logic and ethics. He set himself to accomplish his divine mission by systematic questioning, in the course of which he not only cleared his opponents' minds of much muddle and misconception, but developed his own two important contributions to logic, namely adduction * and general definition. What he did was this. As soon as a term like Courage cropped up in the course of a conversation, he began by asking what it meant; and then, when the attempted answers proved to be unsatisfactory, proceeded to adduce various instances of courage, and show that, though different in detail, they have some common characteristic by which they are all recognizable as what they are; and this, expressed in words, is the definition. All this may seem obvious now, but it had never been made clear before; and it had a most important effect on both logic and metaphysics. It led, through the genius of Plato and Aristotle, to the discovery and distinction of such concepts as quality, substance, essence, attribute, matter and form, genus and species, and innumerable others.

Socrates' direct contribution to the development of philosophy probably ended at this point. He frequently insists that he is not a teacher: that he merely possesses an intellectual skill, analogous to his mother's midwifery, which enables him to help others to bring their thoughts to birth. This might be attributed to the celebrated irony by which he is supposed to have regularly belittled his own knowledge and attainments; but Socrates' disclaimers, even if they contained some exaggeration – and he certainly enjoyed pulling people's legs a little – were probably quite sincere; really honest thinkers are seldom impressed by their own ability. The companions by whom he was constantly surrounded were not so much disciples as friends who loved him and drew inspiration from him. There were others who took pleasure in sharpening their wits against his; others who felt fascinated by him without exactly knowing why; and a loosely attached body of supporters who came mainly for the amusement of hearing his opponents discomfited. Among these last were a number of irresponsible young aristocrats, whose association

* A better word for the Socratic method than 'induction', which has a more technical meaning.

with Socrates did much in the end to provoke his trial and execution. But one young aristocrat was among those who loved him most.

*

Plato was some forty years younger than Socrates, and must have known him from a very early age, because his maternal uncle Charmides and great-uncle Critias were members of the Socratic circle before he was born. Both these men were prominent in the board of extreme oligarchs (called 'the thirty tyrants') which ruled Athens in 404. Also his stepfather Pyrilampes had been closely associated with Pericles. With these connexions it was natural that he should look forward to a political career; but he became disillusioned, first by the example of Critias and Charmides (who earned deep hatred and were killed in civil war) and secondly by the execution of his master under the restored democracy. In any case the influence of Socrates was so powerful that he devoted himself to philosophy, though he never lost sight of its practical bearing upon education and administration, as is clear both from his activities and from his writings. But we are concerned not with his later career but with his relation to Socrates.

The death of Socrates seems to have filled Plato with a passionate desire to preserve and protect his memory. Being a poet – he is the author of some of the most beautiful love-poems in the Greek Anthology – he turned naturally to some form of literary expression; but instead of composing poems about Socrates he conceived the idea of writing dramatic conversations, in which Socrates was represented as employing the same methods of argument which he had used when he was alive.* At first Plato may have written them simply to relieve his own feelings, and they may have been substantially accurate records of actual conversations. But they were circulated and acquired some popularity, and he decided to use them not only to perpetuate Socrates' memory but to vindicate it. For this purpose he wrote the *Apology* and *Crito*. Although the *Euthyphro* precedes them in dramatic order, it was almost certainly written after them; and for this as well as other reasons it seems better to treat them first.

* Some of these dialogues may have been written before Socrates' death, but it seems very improbable.

The *Apology,* although it contains some imaginary dialogue, is not written in dialogue form; it professes to be the speech (or rather series of speeches) delivered by Socrates at his trial. There can be little doubt that it is a faithful record in substance, however much its form owes to Plato's artistry; it would have been stupid to misrepresent facts which were familiar to a great part of the Athenian people. The *Crito* too may be accepted as closely founded upon fact, although the conversation may well be a dramatic summary of arguments with several friends on different occasions. But this is unimportant; the object of the dialogue is clearly to explain and justify Socrates' attitude towards escape, for the benefit of those friends who felt that he had sacrificed himself (and them) too easily – and also of course to display his scorn for subterfuge and his loyal obedience to constitutional authority. The guilt for his condemnation is attached not to the State or to its laws, but to those enemies who have perverted justice.

The *Euthyphro* supplies a sort of prologue to the drama. It shows us Socrates awaiting his trial, and informs us of the charges preferred against him. Strict historicity probably ends here. Euthyphro is no doubt a real person, like the other named characters in Plato's dialogues (though he does not much resemble the Euthyphro who is mentioned in the *Charmides*); but it is unnecessary to believe that he really prosecuted his father for manslaughter in the circumstances that Plato describes. Whether the story is true or not, the artistic purpose is obvious: it presents in an acute form the problem of what piety really is. In the course of the discussion, although the basic absurdity of the charge against Socrates becomes sufficiently plain, we are reminded that his claim to be receptive of supernatural warnings, and his reluctance to accept the cruder features of inherited beliefs about the gods, might easily provoke a suspicion of heterodoxy; and we are reminded also, by a practical example, how disconcerting it was for a professed expert to have his pretensions refuted. But the dialogue does much more than illustrate Socrates' methods and suggest grounds for his unpopularity. Although the discussion apparently fails in its object, it not only considers from various aspects the right attitude of man towards God, but also offers to a thoughtful reader plain indications of what that attitude should be. At the same time (half incidentally, as is Plato's way) important contributions to logical theory are made: genus and species, essence and accident are distinguished, and a good deal of light is thrown upon the proper method of seeking a definition. Altogether it is a most instructive dialogue.

*

The *Phaedo* is a later work and presents a fresh problem. It appears simply to carry the story to its conclusion by narrating, through the mouth of an eye-witness, the events and discussions of the last day in Socrates' life, and the manner of his death. Most people will agree that the opening and closing sections are impregnably authentic. But in the discussion about immortality we find Socrates expressing views which are, to say the least, much more original than anything which we have attributed to him so far. In particular, he not only makes use of the Theory of Forms (or 'Ideas') and its corollary, the doctrine of Recollection, but refers to them as already familiar to his circle, in outline if not in detail. Hence some distinguished authorities, feeling it to be inartistic as well as dishonest (and in the *Phaedo* irreverent too) to put into Socrates' mouth doctrines which he never held, have maintained strongly that Plato's account must be literally true: that whatever Plato's Socrates says was said, or at least could have been said, by the historical Socrates. This view is in itself reasonable and deserves respect; but the balance of evidence is heavily against it, and it is now generally rejected. There is not space here to examine both sides of the case; it is only possible to outline the orthodox position.

It is well known that in the ancient world the work of pupils or followers of great men was often freely attributed to the great men themselves; not necessarily from dishonesty or lack of discrimination, but as a pious acknowledgement of ultimate authorship. We may instance the ascription of the Pentateuch to Moses or the Psalms to David, or in Greece of epic poems and hymns to Homer. Similarly in art many large paintings or sculptured groups are even now regarded as fundamentally the work of the master who conceived the design, even if the execution was left to other hands. In the history of Greek thought Pythagoras certainly and Democritus probably received credit for much that was really the work of their 'schools'. In view of this, is it unnatural that Plato, who undoubtedly felt (at any rate while his influence was still recent) that he was little more than Socrates' mouthpiece, should have represented his revered master as the author of a theory which was largely implicit in his actual methods of debate?

In his attempts to define, Socrates had shown that the same general characteristic is shared by many individual things which, though differing from one another, all have the same 'look'. Apples, turnips, peas, and balls all 'look' round – some more so than others, but they are all instances of roundness – and it is this 'look' (which need not of course be a visible characteristic) which we describe by the definition. Plato, it seems, took this Socratic discovery and carried it further with the help of other suggestions. One of these came from the philosopher Heraclitus, who had stressed the impermanence of everything in the world around us, and the impossibility of *knowing* anything that is changing all the time even as you think of it; yet had insisted that there is an orderly explanation of the apparent confusion. Another came from Parmenides, who taught that *what is* must be changeless and eternal, and that only *what is* can be known. There were others too, but these were the most important.

Plato's reasoning may have been something like this. 'Knowledge must be possible; Socrates was sure of it, and the world makes nonsense if it is not. But the things of this world cannot be truly known, because they are changeable and imperfect, and therefore not real; for *what is* is changeless. Now in geometry [for Plato was an expert mathematician] the properties which we know and can prove to be true of circles and triangles and so on are not strictly true of this particular figure which I draw, because it too is imperfect and impermanent. They are true of the "look" or Form of circle (or triangle), which exists somewhere in eternal perfection. Surely it must be the same with everything else. The things of this world are all imperfect copies of Forms which exist externally somewhere; which are the true and only objects of knowledge, but can only be apprehended by direct contemplation of the mind, freed as far as possible from the confusing imperfections of the physical world.'

This account is not only conjectural but over-simplified. It is merely an attempt to give a sketch of the theory and to show that it may have grown out of Socrates' own beliefs in such a way as to seem no more than a logical extension of them.

Plato modified and developed the theory considerably as time went on, but for the purpose of understanding the *Phaedo* it is only necessary to be clear about a few main points. The Forms are *not* mere concepts (hence the traditional alternative name 'Ideas' is undesirable, as being misleading); they are ultimate facts, intelligible to our minds but quite independent of them. The things of our sensible world exist in a secondary sense, only in so far as they approximate to the corresponding Forms. They are effects of which the Forms are causes, although the precise relation is difficult to describe. It is generally expressed by one of two metaphors: 'imitation', the relation of copy to pattern, and 'participation', the relation of part to whole. A third metaphor, military in origin (but this is not always easy to convey in translation) is regularly used in the *Phaedo* to describe the acquisition of a characteristic: the object is said to 'admit' or 'receive' the Form, and the Form to 'occupy' or 'take possession of' the object. Such figurative language is not a sign of vagueness or incoherence; it is unavoidable when new thoughts have to be expressed.

There is little else in the *Phaedo* that is not self-explanatory. The physchological outlook is simple and Socratic*: man is made up of two parts, physical and psychical, body and soul; and the latter must be cultivated at the expense of the former. This doctrine, and the whole tone of the dialogue, may seem unduly ascetic, especially to those who hope to make the best of both worlds. There certainly appears at first sight to be a strong contrast with the views of the *Symposium,* which has been thought to be a kind of recantation. But the two pictures are really complementary; it is only the viewpoint and emphasis that are different. There is one ultimate question to be faced: Which matters most – body or soul? And there is only one answer.

*

In reading Plato's dialogues it is necessary always to keep in mind the fact – obvious but often forgotten – that they are *not* systematic expositions of his own (or anyone else's) doctrines. This sort of instruction he gave only by word of mouth to his own professed students. The dialogues are works of art, com-

---

* Elsewhere (in the *Republic* and *Phaedrus*) Plato distinguishes three aspects of the soul; but here such an analysis would only confuse the issue.

posed at various times and for special reasons at which we can only guess: partly to release a creative impulse, as one writes a poem or a play; partly to expose a current misapprehension or throw light upon a special problem, as one writes a letter to the newspapers; partly to arouse general interest and guide opinion, as one writes an essay. It is seldom, except in his latest works, that we find any approximation to a formal lecture.

The Athenians enjoyed any kind of debate – it was one of their chief recreations to attend the Assembly and the courts – and they were keen critics of technique. Plato knew this very well; he also knew that different methods appeal to different minds; and, although he condemned the irresponsible use of rhetoric, to produce his effects he used every kind of appeal and every resource of language. Not every argument is closely reasoned; some are merely formal, some 'common-sense', some almost flippant. Natural conversation passes into staccato question-and-answer or a chain of inference in virtual monologue; there are discourses and recapitulations and descriptive or dramatic interludes. The style and diction are now easy, now technical, now eloquent; almost lyrical in the *Phaedo* myth, austerely simple in the great closing scene.

To reproduce this variety of style and tone in English is an almost impossible task. The present translation does not claim to be successful, although it owes much to the helpful criticism of my friends and colleagues Dr J. M. S. Tompkins and Miss Avery Woodward, and to suggestions (on points of emphasis and dramatic interpretation) made by Mr Rayner Heppenstall during the broadcast of selections in the B.B.C.'s Third Programme.

HUGH TREDENNICK

NOTE: *The figures and letters printed at the top of each right-hand page of the translation refer to the pagination of the 1578 edition of Plato by Henri Estienne (Stephanus). References to Plato's text are regularly made in this way.*

SOCRATES IN ACTION

Outside the court-house where he is shortly to stand his trial Socrates meets Euthyphro, a seer and religious expert, who says that he is going to charge his own father with manslaughter. Socrates is startled, and inquires how Euthyphro can be sure that such conduct is consistent with his religious duty. The result is a discussion of the true nature of Piety. (As this subject does not often arise in present-day conversation, it is not always easy to find simple and natural English equivalents for the ideas put forward in the discussion. 'Piety' itself may offend some ears; but no better word seems to be available.)

Euthyphro does not represent Athenian orthodoxy; on the contrary, he is sympathetic towards Socrates. He is an independent specialist, confident in his own infallibility, and therefore a fit subject for Socrates' curative treatment, which aims at clearing the mind of false assumptions and so making it receptive of real knowledge. Such treatment is irksome to the patient, but Euthyphro (for all his pomposity) takes it in good part; he does not even mind Socrates' gentle teasing – or perhaps he is unconscious of it. Nor is Socrates' attitude purely negative: he means to help his friend to a better way of thinking; and although the argument moves in a circle, it offers clues for the solution of the problem.

EUTHYPHRO

EUTHYPHRO: What revolution has taken place in your affairs, Socrates, that you have left your usual haunts in the Lyceum[1] and are now spending your time here waiting about the porch of the King Archon?[2] I don't suppose that you have actually got a case before the King Archon, as I have.

SOCRATES: No, Euthyphro; the official name for it is not a private case but a public action.

EUTHYPHRO: Really? I suppose that someone has brought an action against you; I won't insult you by suggesting that you have done it to somebody else.

SOCRATES: No, I haven't.

EUTHYPHRO: But somebody else has done it to you?

SOCRATES: Exactly.

EUTHYPHRO: Who is he?

SOCRATES: I don't even know him very well myself, Euthyphro; he seems to be a young man and undistinguished; but I believe he is called Meletus.[3] He belongs to the parish of Pitthis – if you can think of a Meletus of Pitthis with long straight hair and a thinnish beard and a rather beaky nose.

EUTHYPHRO: I don't recall him, Socrates. But tell me, what sort of action has he brought against you?

SOCRATES: What sort? Not a trivial one, as I see it; it's no small achievement to have made such an important discovery at his age. He claims to know how the characters of the young get corrupted, and who the people are that are responsible. I expect that he's a clever fellow, who has observed my ignorance and is coming forward to denounce me to the State for corrupting his contemporaries – like a little boy telling his mother. It seems to me that he is the only one of our politicians who is beginning in the right way; because the right way is to give one's

attention first to the highest good of the young, just as
you expect a good gardener to give his attention first to
the young plants, and after that to the others. In the
same way, no doubt, Meletus is first clearing out us
pests who, according to him, spoil the tender shoots of the
young; and then after that he will obviously turn his attention to the older generation, and so become the author
of countless incalculable benefits to the State. At any
rate that would be the natural result from such a beginning.

EUTHYPHRO: I should wish it to be so, Socrates, but I am
very much afraid that the opposite will happen. It
seems to me that in trying to injure you he is simply
beginning to ruin our city at its very heart. Tell me,
what are the activities by which he asserts that you
corrupt the young?

SOCRATES: Absurd ones, my very good friend; at any
rate on the first hearing. He says that I am an inventor of
gods;[4] and it is precisely because I invent new gods and
don't acknowledge the old ones that he has brought this
action against me – so he says.

EUTHYPHRO: I see, Socrates; it's because of your saying
that you are constantly visited by your supernatural
voice. So he has indicted you for introducing unorthodox views; and he is coming into court to misrepresent
your conduct, because he knows that it is easy to misrepresent this sort of thing to the masses. Why, you
know, even in my own case when, in predicting the
future,[5] I make some statement about religion to them in
the Assembly, they laugh at me as if I were crazy; and
yet I have never predicted a word that wasn't true; but it
makes no difference – they are jealous of all of us who
possess these qualities. Still, we mustn't let them worry
us, but close with them boldly.

SOCRATES: But, my dear Euthyphro, just being laughed at
is presumably nothing to worry about. It seems to me,
you know, that the people of Athens are very little con-

cerned if they think that a person is an expert, provided that he doesn't try to impart his cleverness. It's when they think that somebody is making others as clever as himself that they get angry – perhaps through jealousy, as you suggest, or for some other reason.

EUTHYPHRO: Then I'm not at all anxious to test their feelings towards *me* in that respect.

SOCRATES: You needn't worry, because probably they feel that you seldom show yourself in public, and have no wish to impart your wisdom; but for my own part I am afraid that they assume, because of my sociable nature, that I open my mind unreservedly to everyone, not only without charging a fee[6] but in perfect readiness to pay one, if anyone is willing to listen to me. So, as I said just now, if they only intended to laugh at me, as you say they do at you, it wouldn't be at all unpleasant to spend our time in the law-court joking and laughing. But if they are going to be serious, then there's no knowing how the case will turn out – except for you prophets.

EUTHYPHRO: I dare say that it will come to nothing, Socrates, and you will conduct your case satisfactorily, as I expect to conduct mine.

SOCRATES: Oh yes, Euthyphro, what is this lawsuit of yours? are you defending yourself or prosecuting?

EUTHYPHRO: Prosecuting.

SOCRATES: Whom?

EUTHYPHRO: Someone by prosecuting whom I am increasing my reputation for craziness.

SOCRATES: Why, is he such a nimble opponent?[7]

EUTHYPHRO: Not at all nimble; actually he's quite an old gentleman.

SOCRATES: Who is this person?

EUTHYPHRO: My father.

SOCRATES: My good man! your own father?

EUTHYPHRO: Yes, indeed.

SOCRATES: What is the charge? what is the trial for?

EUTHYPHRO: Manslaughter, Socrates.

SOCRATES: Good heavens! Of course, most people have
no idea, Euthyphro, what the rights of such a case
are. I imagine that it isn't everyone that may take such a
course, but only one who is far advanced in wisdom.

EUTHYPHRO: Far indeed, Socrates.

SOCRATES: Well, is the person that your father has killed
a member of your own household? – Obviously he is;
you wouldn't, of course, be prosecuting him for killing
an outsider.

EUTHYPHRO: It is funny that you should think that it
makes any difference, Socrates, whether the dead man
was an outsider or a member of my own household, and
not realize that the only point at issue is whether the
killer killed lawfully or not; and that if he did, he must
be let alone, but if he did not, he must be prosecuted –
that is, if he is a sharer of your hearth and table; because
if you consciously associate with such a person and do
not purify yourself and him by prosecuting him at law,
you share equally in the pollution of his guilt.[8] As a
matter of fact, the deceased was a day-labourer of mine;
we were farming in Naxos[9] and he was working for us
there. Well, he got drunk, lost his temper with one of
our servants, and knifed him. So my father bound him
hand and foot and threw him into a ditch; and then sent
a man over here to ask the proper authority[10] what was
to be done. In the meanwhile he not only troubled himself very little about the prisoner but neglected him altogether, considering that he was a murderer, and it would
not matter if he died. And that was just what happened;
what with starvation and exposure and confinement, he
died before the messenger came back from consulting the
expert. That is why both my father and my other relations are angry with me: because on the murderer's
account I am prosecuting my father for manslaughter,
whereas in the first place (as they maintain) he did not
kill the man, and in the second, even supposing that he

did kill him, since the dead man was a murderer, one ought not to concern one's self in defence of such a person, because it is an act of impiety for a son to prosecute his father for manslaughter. They have a poor comprehension, Socrates, of how the divine law stands with regard to piety and impiety.

SOCRATES: But tell me, Euthyphro, do you really believe that you understand the ruling of the divine law, and what makes actions pious and impious, so accurately that in the circumstances that you describe you have no misgivings? aren't you afraid that in taking your father into court you may turn out to be committing an act of impiety yourself?

EUTHYPHRO: No, Socrates; I shouldn't be worth much, and Euthyphro would be no better than the common run of men, if I didn't have accurate knowledge about all that sort of thing.

SOCRATES: In that case, Euthyphro, since you have this remarkable talent, the best thing I can do, I suppose, is to become your pupil; and before Meletus' case against me comes on, to challenge him upon this very point, saying that even in the past I was eager for knowledge about religion; and now, since he asserts that I am grievously at fault in my independent thinking and unorthodox views about religion, I have become your pupil. 'And if you admit, Meletus,' I would say, 'that Euthyphro is an expert in such matters, you must suppose that my beliefs are true too, and drop your case against me. If you don't admit it, then before you bring an accusation against me you must bring one against him, my teacher, for corrupting the elderly, myself and his own father – myself by his teaching, and his father by admonition and correction.' And if he refuses to listen and doesn't drop the case against me or indict you instead, I suppose I had better repeat the same challenge in court. Is that right?

EUTHYPHRO: Upon my word, Socrates, if he really tried to

indict me, I fancy I should find his weak spot; and we should have had our say about him in court long before he had his about me!

SOCRATES: I realize that as well as you do, my dear friend; and that's why I am anxious to become your pupil, because I know that this person Meletus (there are others, no doubt, but Meletus in particular) seems not even to notice *you,* whereas he has marked *me* down so easily with his sharp eyes that he has indicted me for impiety. So now I appeal to you to tell me what you were insisting just now that you definitely know: what you mean by piety and impiety, both in respect of manslaughter and in all other connexions. Isn't it true that in every action piety is self-identical, and similarly impiety is in every instance the opposite of piety, but consistent with itself; in other words that everything that is to be regarded as impious has a single definite characteristic[11] in respect of its impiety?

EUTHYPHRO: No doubt that is quite true, Socrates.

SOCRATES: Then tell me, how do you define piety and impiety?

EUTHYPHRO: Very well; I say that piety consists in just what I am doing now: prosecuting a wrongdoer for manslaughter or temple-robbery or any other such crime, whether the offender happens to be your father or your mother or anybody else; and that not to prosecute such a person is impious.[12] I will quote you a piece of evidence, Socrates – I have already pointed it out to others in justification of my conduct – to show that this is how the law stands: I mean that one must not give in to the doer of an impious action, no matter who he may be. And observe what weighty evidence it is. People really believe of their own accord that Zeus is the best and most righteous of all the gods; and at the same time they agree that he put his father in chains for swallowing his sons in defiance of the right, and that his father correspondingly mutilated *his* father on similar grounds.[13] Yet they take me to task for prosecuting my father when he does wrong, thus contradicting themselves by laying down one rule for the gods and another for me.

SOCRATES: Do you think that is the reason why I am being called to trial, Euthyphro, because when I hear anyone telling stories like these about the gods I somehow find it difficult to accept them? Naturally that will make it said that my views are quite wrong. So now if you, who are an expert in this sort of thing, also believe these stories, I suppose that people like myself must assent too.[14] What is there for us to say, when we ourselves admit that we know nothing about the subject? But tell me, in friendship's name, do you really believe that these things happened as they are described?

EUTHYPHRO: Yes, and things still more wonderful, Socrates, which ordinary people don't know.

SOCRATES: So you believe too that there really is civil war among the gods, and violent quarrels and fights, and a great deal more of the same kind? I mean the sort of thing that the poets[15] describe and the master artists portray in their religious pictures, especially on the robe which is carried up to the Acropolis at the great Panathenaic festival,[16] and which is simply covered with such representations; are we to say that these stories are true, Euthyphro?

EUTHYPHRO: Yes, Socrates, and not only these, but (as I said just now) if you like I will tell you a great many other facts about our religion, which will astonish you, I'm sure, when you hear them.

SOCRATES: I shouldn't be surprised. But you shall tell me about them some other time when we have leisure; at the moment I want you to try to answer more precisely the question that I put to you just now. You see, my friend, when I asked you before what piety was, you didn't tell me enough; you said that what you are doing now –

prosecuting your father for manslaughter – was a pious action.

EUTHYPHRO: Yes, and what I said was true, Socrates.

SOCRATES: No doubt; but surely you admit that there are many other actions that are pious.

EUTHYPHRO: So there are.

SOCRATES: Well, then, do you recollect that what I urged you to do was not to tell me about one or two of these many pious actions, but to describe the actual feature that makes all pious actions pious? – because you said, I believe, that impious actions are impious, and similarly pious ones pious, in virtue of a single characteristic. Or don't you remember?

EUTHYPHRO: Yes, I do.

SOCRATES: Then explain to me what this characteristic is in itself, so that by fixing my eyes upon it and using it as a pattern [17] I may be able to describe any action, yours or anyone else's, as pious if it corresponds to the pattern and impious if it doesn't.

EUTHYPHRO: If that's how you want your answer, Socrates, that's how I will give it.

SOCRATES: That *is* how I want it.

EUTHYPHRO: Very well, then; what is agreeable to the gods is pious, and what is disagreeable to them impious.

SOCRATES: An excellent answer, Euthyphro, and in just the form that I wanted. [18] Whether it is true I don't know yet; but no doubt you will go on to make it clear to me that your statement is correct.

EUTHYPHRO: Certainly.

SOCRATES: Come along then; let's consider what we are saying. The action or person that is god-beloved [19] is pious, and the action or person that is god-hated is impious, piety being not the same as impiety but its direct opposite. Isn't that our position?

EUTHYPHRO: Yes, it is.

SOCRATES: And the definition seems satisfactory?

EUTHYPHRO: I think so, Socrates

SOCRATES: Haven't we also said that the gods are divided, Euthyphro, and disagree with one another, and feel enmity towards one another?

EUTHYPHRO: Yes, we have.

SOCRATES: What sort of disagreement is it, my good friend, that causes enmity and anger? Let us look at it in this way. If you and I disagreed about the question which of two numbers was the greater, would this disagreement make us hostile and angry with one another? Shouldn't we quickly settle a dispute of this kind by having recourse to arithmetic?

EUTHYPHRO: Certainly.

SOCRATES: And supposing that we disagreed about the relative size of two objects, shouldn't we quickly put an end to our quarrel by having recourse to measurement?

EUTHYPHRO: Quite so.

SOCRATES: And I presume that we should decide a question of relative weight by having recourse to weighing?

EUTHYPHRO: Of course.

SOCRATES: Then what would be the subject of dispute about which we should be unable to reach agreement, so that we became hostile to one another and lost our tempers? Very likely you can't say off-hand; but consider, as I suggest them, whether the required subjects are questions of right and wrong, honour and dishonour, good and bad. Isn't it when we disagree about these, and can't reach a satisfactory decision about them, that we become hostile to one another (when we do become hostile) – both you and I and all the rest of mankind?

EUTHYPHRO: Yes, that is the sort of disagreement, Socrates: about the subjects that you mention.

SOCRATES: And what about the gods, Euthyphro? If they do disagree at all, won't it be for just these reasons?

EUTHYPHRO: Quite inevitably.

SOCRATES: Then on your view, my worthy Euthyphro, it follows that the gods too hold different opinions about

27

what is right, and similarly about what is honourable and dishonourable, good and bad; because surely they would not be divided if they didn't disagree on these subjects. Isn't that so?

EUTHYPHRO: You are quite right.

SOCRATES: Then does each faction love what it considers to be honourable and good and right, and hate the opposite?

EUTHYPHRO: Certainly.

SOCRATES: But according to you the same things are regarded by some of the gods as right and by others as wrong; I mean the things about which they dispute and so are divided and fight one another. Isn't that so?

EUTHYPHRO: Yes.

SOCRATES: So apparently the same things are both loved and hated by the gods; that is, the same things will be both god-beloved and god-hated.

EUTHYPHRO: Apparently.

SOCRATES: Then by this argument, Euthyphro, the same things will also be both pious and impious.

EUTHYPHRO: Perhaps so.

SOCRATES: Then you didn't answer my question, my talented friend. I didn't ask you to tell me something which is actually at once both pious and impious; and apparently what is god-beloved is also god-hated. So with regard to your present action in correcting your father, Euthyphro, it would not be surprising if in doing this you are doing what is agreeable to Zeus but offensive to Cronos and Uranus, and pleasing to Hephaestus but offensive to Hera; [20] and similarly with any other gods who disagree with one another on the subject.

EUTHYPHRO: But I imagine, Socrates, that none of the gods disagrees with one another on this point, at any rate: that whoever kills without justification should be brought to justice.

SOCRATES: Then tell me this, Euthyphro: in the case of human beings, have you never heard anyone disputing that a man who has killed unjustly or committed some other crime ought to be punished?

EUTHYPHRO: On the contrary, they never stop disputing these questions, especially in the law-courts. They commit any number of crimes, and then go to all lengths in word and deed to escape punishment.

SOCRATES: Do they actually admit that they are guilty, Euthyphro, and yet in spite of their admission claim that they ought not to be punished?

EUTHYPHRO: No, not that, of course.

SOCRATES: Then they don't go to *all* lengths; because there is one thing, I suppose, that they don't dare to say: they don't dispute that *if* they are guilty they ought to be punished, but presumably they deny that they are guilty, don't they?

EUTHYPHRO: That is true.

SOCRATES: So they do not dispute that a guilty person ought to be punished; what they probably *do* dispute is who the guilty person is, and what he does, and when he does it.

EUTHYPHRO: That is true.

SOCRATES: Then are not the gods in exactly the same position – assuming that they are divided about questions of right and wrong, as you make out – some accusing one another of doing wrong, and others denying it? because surely nobody, my talented friend, whether god or man, dares to maintain that one ought not to be punished if he *is* guilty.

EUTHYPHRO: Yes, what you say is true, Socrates; in the main, at any rate.

SOCRATES: But I imagine, Euthyphro, that each single act is disputed by the disputants, whether they are men or gods – assuming that the gods do dispute. It is because they disagree about some action that some say it has been done rightly and others wrongly. Isn't that so?

EUTHYPHRO: Quite.

SOCRATES: Come along, then, my dear Euthyphro; impart your knowledge to me, so that I may become wiser. If a hired labourer commits murder, and is tied up by the master of the man he has killed, and dies because of his bonds before the man who tied him up discovers from the authorities what the proper procedure is, what evidence have you that *all* the gods regard this man as wrongfully done to death, and that on behalf of such a person it is right for a son to prosecute his father and denounce him for manslaughter? Come, try to give me some definite proof that in these circumstances beyond all doubt all the gods regard this action as right; and if you prove it to my satisfaction, I shall never stop singing the praises of your wisdom.

EUTHYPHRO: It would probably be no light undertaking, Socrates. Of course I *could* demonstrate it quite plainly.

SOCRATES: I see; you say that because you think that I am duller than the jury. Obviously you will prove to *them* both that these acts are wrong and that the gods one and all detest such doings.

EUTHYPHRO: Quite definitely, Socrates, provided that they listen to what I say.

SOCRATES: Oh yes, they will listen, provided that they think your case is well presented. But a thought occurred to me just as you were speaking, and I am turning it over in my mind, like this. 'Even supposing that Euthyphro made it perfectly plain to me that the gods one and all regard this sort of homicide as wrong, how much has he helped me to understand what piety and impiety mean? This deed may well, as it appears, be god-hated. But in point of fact we did not find just now that this is the distinction between what is pious and what is not; we found that what is god-hated is also god-beloved.' So I concede you the nature of your father's action, Euthyphro; let us assume, if you like, that all gods regard it as wrong and detest it. But suppose that we now make a correction in our formula, to the effect that what *all* the gods hate is impious and what they *all* love is pious (whereas what some love and others hate is neither or both); is this how you would like our definition to stand now with regard to piety and impiety?

EUTHYPHRO: What is there against it, Socrates?

SOCRATES: Nothing on my part, Euthyphro; but I want you to consider on yours whether this assumption will make it easiest for you to instruct me as you promised.

EUTHYPHRO: Very well; I should say that piety is what all the gods love, and that the opposite, what all the gods hate, is impiety.

SOCRATES: Should we then consider this definition in its turn, Euthyphro, to see whether it is satisfactory, or should we let it pass and simply accept both our own and other people's assumptions, taking the speaker's mere word for the truth of what he says? Shouldn't we examine the implications of his statement?

EUTHYPHRO: Yes, we should. All the same, I think that this definition is now satisfactory.

SOCRATES: We shall soon be better able to judge, my good sir. Consider this question: is what is pious loved by the gods because it is pious, or is it pious because it is loved? [21]

EUTHYPHRO: I don't understand what you mean, Socrates.

SOCRATES: Well, I will try to explain more clearly. Do we speak of things as *carried* and *carrying*, *led* and *leading*, *seen* and *seeing*? and do you understand that in all such pairs of terms each is different from the other, and in what way they are different? [22]

EUTHYPHRO: Yes, I think I understand.

SOCRATES: Is there also something that is *loved* and something else that is *loving*?

EUTHYPHRO: Of course.

SOCRATES: Tell me, then: is a carried thing carried because one carries it, or for some other reason?

EUTHYPHRO: No; the reason is just that.

SOCRATES: And a led thing is led because one leads it, and a seen thing seen because one sees it?

EUTHYPHRO: Certainly.

SOCRATES: So we don't see a thing because it is a seen thing, but on the contrary it is a seen thing because we see it; and we don't lead a thing because it is a led thing, but it is a led thing because we lead it; and we don't carry a thing because it is a carried thing, but it is a carried thing because we carry it. Is my meaning quite plain, Euthyphro? What I mean is this: that if anything is produced, or acted upon in any way, it is not produced because it is a product, but it is a product because it is produced;[23] and it is not acted upon because it is the object of an action, but it is the object of an action because it is acted upon. Don't you agree that this is so?

EUTHYPHRO: Yes, I do.

SOCRATES: Well, then, isn't a loved thing either a product or the object of some action?

EUTHYPHRO: Certainly.

SOCRATES: So it is the same with this as with our earlier examples: it is not loved by those who love it because it is an object of love, but it is an object of love because it is loved.

EUTHYPHRO: Yes, that must be so.

SOCRATES: Then what do we say about piety? Isn't it loved by all the gods, according to your definition?

EUTHYPHRO: Yes.

SOCRATES: Just because it is pious, or for some other reason?

EUTHYPHRO: No; because it is pious.

SOCRATES: So it is loved because it is pious, not pious because it is loved?

EUTHYPHRO: It seems so.

SOCRATES: But it is because a thing is loved by the gods that it is an object of love or god-beloved.

EUTHYPHRO: Of course.

SOCRATES: Then what is god-beloved is not the same as

what is pious, Euthyphro, nor is what is pious the same as what is god-beloved, as you assert; they are two different things.

EUTHYPHRO: How do you make that out, Socrates?

SOCRATES: Because we agree that what is pious is loved because it is pious, and not pious because it is loved; isn't that so?

EUTHYPHRO: Yes.

SOCRATES: And we agree that what is god-beloved is god-beloved because the gods love it, from the very fact of their loving it; and that they do not love it because it is god-beloved.

EUTHYPHRO: That is true.

SOCRATES: But if what is god-beloved were identical with what is pious, my dear Euthyphro, then if what is pious were loved because it is pious, what is god-beloved would be loved because it is god-beloved; and if what is god-beloved were god-beloved because it is loved by the gods, then what is pious would be pious because it is loved by them. As it is, you can see that the relation between them is just the opposite; which shows that they are entirely different from each other. The one is lovable because it is loved, and the other is loved because it is lovable. I rather think, Euthyphro, that when I asked you what piety is you were unwilling to disclose its essence to me, and merely stated one of its attributes,[24] saying that piety has the attribute of being loved by all the gods; but you have not yet told me what it is that has this attribute. So, if you have no objection, please don't conceal the truth from me, but make a fresh start and tell me what piety *is* that it is loved by the gods or has any other attribute – we shan't quarrel about that –; tell me without reserve what piety and impiety are.

EUTHYPHRO: But, Socrates, I don't know how to convey to you what I have in mind. Whatever we put forward somehow keeps on shifting its position and refuses to stay where we laid it down.

SOCRATES: Your statements are the handiwork of my ancestor Daedalus,[25] Euthyphro; and if I had been the one that uttered them and laid them down, no doubt you would have poked fun at me by suggesting that it was my relationship to him that made the products of my arguments run away and refuse to stay where they are put. As it is, the propositions are yours, so we need some other witticism; because it is for you that they refuse to stay, as you yourself can see.

EUTHYPHRO: As I see it, Socrates, the witticism that these statements call for is just about the same as you said; because it isn't I that endow them with this faculty of moving about and not staying in the same place, it strikes me that *you* are the Daedalus, because so far as I am concerned they would have stayed as they were.

SOCRATES: In that case, my dear fellow, it looks as though I were a greater genius in my art than Daedalus was; he only gave his own works the power of movement, whereas I apparently give it to other people's as well as my own. And please note that the most intriguing feature of my art is that my ingenuity is unintentional. I would rather that our statements held good and were firmly established than have the wealth of Tantalus [26] as well as the skill of Daedalus. But enough of this. Since you seem to be demoralized,[27] I myself will help you to make the effort to instruct me about piety; and don't give up prematurely. Now consider whether it doesn't seem to you that everything pious must be morally right.

EUTHYPHRO: Yes, it does.

SOCRATES: Then is everything that is morally right pious? Isn't the truth that, although what is pious is all morally right, what is morally right is not all pious, but some of it is pious and some is something else?

EUTHYPHRO: I don't follow your meaning, Socrates.

SOCRATES: And yet you are quite as much younger [28] than I am as you are wiser; but, as I said, you are demoralized by your wealth of wisdom. I'm surprised at you; pull

yourself together. As a matter of fact what I mean isn't
difficult to understand either. I maintain the opposite of
what the poet [29] said who wrote

> But Zeus the Maker, him who did create
> All this our world, he will not reprehend;
> For where fear is, there too is reverence.

Well, I disagree with this poet. Shall I tell you why?

EUTHYPHRO: Certainly.

SOCRATES: I don't think that it is true to say that where
there is fear there is also reverence. It seems to me that
there are plenty of people who fear disease and poverty
and any number of other such misfortunes, and who, in
spite of their fear, feel not the slightest reverence for
what they fear. Don't you agree?

EUTHYPHRO: Certainly.

SOCRATES: But I think that it *is* true that where reverence
is, there fear is also. Is there anyone who feels diffidence
and shame at some action and does not at the same time
fear and dread a reputation for wrongdoing?

EUTHYPHRO: No; he fears too.

SOCRATES: Then it is not correct to say 'for where fear is,
there too is reverence'. Where there is reverence there is
fear, but there is not reverence everywhere that there is
fear, because fear presumably has a wider extension than
reverence. Reverence is a kind of fear, just as 'odd' is a
kind of number; so that there is not 'odd' wherever there
is number, but there is number wherever there is 'odd'.
You follow me now, I suppose?

EUTHYPHRO: Certainly.

SOCRATES: Well, that's what I meant when I asked you a
short time ago: Is there piety wherever there is moral
rectitude? Isn't the truth really that where there is piety
there is rectitude, but where there is rectitude there is not
always piety? Shall we assert this view, or do you think
otherwise?

EUTHYPHRO: No, let us assert it; I think that you are
right.

SOCRATES: Then observe the next step. If piety is a kind of moral rectitude, then presumably we ought to discover what kind [30] of moral rectitude piety is. Now if you had been asking me about one of the examples that I mentioned just now, for instance, what kind of number 'even' is, or what is the real nature of this sort of number, I should have said 'Whatever is not scalene but isosceles'. [31] Don't you think so?

EUTHYPHRO: Yes, I do.

SOCRATES: Then I want you to explain to me in the same way what kind of moral rectitude piety is; so that I in my turn may tell Meletus to stop his unfair attack and drop his indictment for irreverence, because I have now been well enough instructed by you to know what is reverent and pious and what is not.

EUTHYPHRO: Well, Socrates, it seems to me that reverence or piety is that kind of rectitude which is concerned with tendance [32] of the gods, and the remaining kind of rectitude is that which is concerned with the tendance of human beings.

SOCRATES: And an excellent answer too, in my opinion, Euthyphro; but I still haven't got quite all that I want, because I'm not sure yet what you mean by tendance. I presume you don't mean by tendance in the case of the gods just the same sort of tendance as in all other uses of the word, because surely we use the term – Well, for instance, we say that not everyone knows how to tend horses, but only the horse-trainer. Isn't that so?

EUTHYPHRO: Certainly.

SOCRATES: Because horse-training is the tendance of horses?

EUTHYPHRO: Yes.

SOCRATES: And in the same way not everyone knows how to tend dogs, but only the dog-trainer.

EUTHYPHRO: Quite so.

SOCRATES: Because dog-training is the tendance of dogs.

EUTHYPHRO: Yes.

SOCRATES: And cattle-farming is the tendance of cattle.

EUTHYPHRO: Certainly.

SOCRATES: Then is piety or reverence the tendance of the gods, Euthyphro? Is that what you mean?

EUTHYPHRO: Yes, it is.

SOCRATES: Isn't the effect of all tendance the same? What I mean is that it is for the good or benefit of the thing tended: as you can see that horses tended by horse-training are benefited and improved. Don't you agree?

EUTHYPHRO: Yes, I do.

SOCRATES: And so, I presume, are dogs by dog-training and cattle by cattle-farming, and so on with all the rest. Or do you think that the tendance aims at the hurt of the thing tended?

EUTHYPHRO: Certainly not.

SOCRATES: It aims at the benefit of it?

EUTHYPHRO: Of course.

SOCRATES: Then if piety is tendance of the gods, is it a benefit to the gods, and does it make them better? Would you agree that when you do a pious act you make some one of the gods better?

EUTHYPHRO: No, certainly not.

SOCRATES: No, Euthyphro, I didn't think that was your meaning either – far from it; that's why I pressed you to explain what sort of tendance of the gods you meant, because I didn't think that you meant this kind.

EUTHYPHRO: And you were quite right, Socrates; I don't mean the kind that you described.

SOCRATES: Very good. Well, what sort of tendance of the gods *do* you mean by piety?

EUTHYPHRO: The same tendance that slaves [33] give their masters, Socrates.

SOCRATES: I see. It would be a sort of service to the gods, I suppose.

EUTHYPHRO: Exactly.

SOCRATES: Then take the case of service rendered by doctors; can you tell me what the object is that the service is actually rendered to achieve? Don't you think it is health?

EUTHYPHRO: Yes, I do.

SOCRATES: And what about the service rendered by ship-wrights? What is the object that this service is rendered to achieve?

EUTHYPHRO: Obviously a ship, Socrates.

SOCRATES: And in the case of builders I suppose it is a house.

EUTHYPHRO: Yes.

SOCRATES: Tell me, then, my good friend, what is the object to achieve which service to the gods would be rendered? Obviously you know, because you claim to have a better knowledge of religion than anyone else.

EUTHYPHRO: Yes, and it is a true claim, Socrates.

SOCRATES: Then tell me, in Heaven's name, what is the supremely splendid work that the gods accomplish by using our services?

EUTHYPHRO: They achieve many splendid results, Socrates.

SOCRATES: So do military commanders, my friend; but all the same one can easily summarize what they do as achieving victory in war. Isn't that so?

EUTHYPHRO: Of course.

SOCRATES: Farmers too achieve many splendid results; but all the same their achievement can be summarized as producing food from the soil.

EUTHYPHRO: Quite so.

SOCRATES: Then what about the many splendid results that the gods achieve? What is the summary of their achievement?

EUTHYPHRO: I did tell you a short time ago, Socrates, that it would be too heavy a task for you to learn in detail how all these matters stand. But this much I can tell you in general. If a man understands how to say and do, in prayer and sacrifice, what is pleasing to the gods, this is piety; and it is this sort of observance that preserves both private households and the public life of states. But the opposite of what is pleasing to the gods is impiety; and it is this that overturns and ruins everything. [34]

SOCRATES: I am sure that you could have given a summary answer to my question in far fewer words, Euthyphro, if you had wanted to. The fact is that you have no inclination to instruct me – that's quite obvious. Why, you veered away then just at the critical moment when, if you had answered me, I should have had by now all the information that I wanted [35] from you about piety. As it is – because the lover must follow step by step wherever his love [36] leads him – tell me, please, what you mean this time by the terms 'pious' and 'piety'; a sort of sacrifice and prayer?

EUTHYPHRO: Yes.

SOCRATES: Doesn't sacrifice consist in making presents to the gods, and prayer in making requests to them?

EUTHYPHRO: Yes, indeed, Socrates.

SOCRATES: So on this view piety would be a science of asking and giving.

EUTHYPHRO: You grasp my meaning perfectly, Socrates.

SOCRATES: You see, my friend, I am a passionate admirer of your wisdom and keep my attention fixed upon it, so that no word of yours will fall to the ground. But tell me, what is this form of service to the gods? Do you hold that it consists in asking from them and giving to them?

EUTHYPHRO: Yes, I do.

SOCRATES: Then would not the right procedure in asking them be to ask for what we need from them?

EUTHYPHRO: What else could it be?

SOCRATES: And similarly would not the right procedure in giving be to present them in return with what they actually need from us? because surely it would be an incompetent use of presents to give a person things for which he has no need.

EUTHYPHRO: Quite true, Socrates.

SOCRATES: So piety would seem, Euthyphro, to be a sort of art of commerce between gods and men.

EUTHYPHRO: Yes, if you like it better to describe it so.

SOCRATES: I don't like it any better unless it is really true. But tell me, what benefit do the gods really get from the gifts that they receive from us? What they give is obvious to anyone, for we have nothing good that they don't give us; but what benefit do they get from what they receive from us? Is our commerce with them so much to our advantage that we receive all our good things from them, while they receive none from us?

EUTHYPHRO: But do you really imagine, Socrates, that the gods derive benefit from the things that they receive from us?

SOCRATES: Well, if not, whatever can these gifts of ours to the gods be, Euthyphro?

EUTHYPHRO: Why, honour and esteem and – as I was saying just now – gratitude; what else do you suppose?

SOCRATES: So piety is what is gratifying to the gods, Euthyphro, but not beneficial nor dear to them?

EUTHYPHRO: In my opinion it is supremely dear to them.

SOCRATES: Then apparently piety is once more what is dear to the gods.

EUTHYPHRO: Absolutely.

SOCRATES: If that's what you say, can you be surprised if your statements visibly shift their ground instead of keeping still? and will you accuse me of being a Daedalus and making them move, when you yourself are a much cleverer craftsman than Daedalus and make them move round in a circle?[37] Don't you see that our discussion has gone right round and come back to the point from which we started? You must surely remember that at an earlier stage[38] we found that piety and what is god-beloved are not the same, but are two different things. Don't you remember?

EUTHYPHRO: Yes, I do.

SOCRATES: Then don't you realize that now you are saying

that piety is what is dear to the gods? And this surely amounts to what is god-beloved, doesn't it?

EUTHYPHRO: Certainly.

SOCRATES: Then either we were wrong in our recent conclusion or, if we were right then, we are mistaken in our present assumption.

EUTHYPHRO: So it seems.

SOCRATES: Then we shall have to start our inquiry about piety all over again from the beginning; because I shall never give up of my own accord until I have learnt the answer. Only don't refuse to take me seriously, but do your best now to give me your closest attention, and tell me the truth; because you know it if any man does, and like Proteus [39] you mustn't be allowed to go until you have spoken. If you didn't know all about piety and impiety you would never have attempted to prosecute your aged father for manslaughter on behalf of a mere labourer; you would have been too much afraid of the gods, and too much ashamed of what men might think, to run such a risk, in case you should be wrong in doing so. As it is, I am sure that you think you know [40] all about what is pious and what is not. So tell me your opinion, my most worthy Euthyphro, and don't conceal it.

EUTHYPHRO: Another time, then, Socrates; at the moment I have an urgent engagement somewhere, and it's time for me to be off.

SOCRATES: What a way to treat me, my friend! Fancy your going off like this and dashing me from my great hope! I thought that if I learnt from you about piety and impiety I should both escape from Meletus' indictment (by demonstrating to him that I had now become instructed by Euthyphro in religion, and no longer in my ignorance expressed independent and unorthodox views) and also live better for the rest of my life. [41]

SOCRATES ON TRIAL

In the year 399 B.C. *three Athenian citizens – Meletus, Anytus, and Lycon – brought a public action against Socrates as being a menace to society.*

The first part of the charge – heresy – was no doubt primarily intended to inflame prejudice. (It had already been used with success against the philosopher Anaxagoras, some of whose views were apparently imputed to Socrates.) It could hardly have been substantiated, because Socrates was punctilious in his religious observances. Still, he may well have pointed out incongruities or unworthy elements in traditional beliefs; and his 'divine voice' could have been represented as the profane invention of a dangerous free-thinker.

The second and more serious part of the charge was that Socrates 'corrupted the minds of the young'. This superficial absurdity had a certain political foundation. His circle included or had included a number of right-wing aristocrats whose memory, even if (like Critias) they were now dead, was still abhorred; and one of his closest pupils had been the brilliant Alcibiades, remembered now only as a traitor who had ruined his country. It was possible to argue that it was Socrates who had led these men astray, and that he was doing the same to others. Also his tendency to regard popular opinion as ignorant made him suspect in the eyes of the democratic party, of which Anytus, the most influential of his accusers, was a prominent member.

Thus the prosecution relied mainly on the powerful conjunction of religious and political hostility. They also counted upon Socrates' unpopularity with those whose self-pride he had offended; and they hoped that his uncompromising attitude would alienate the jury, which expected flattery and abject entreaties.

The procedure in court was as follows. Litigants had to state their own case, without the help of counsel. The prosecution spoke first, and when the defendant had replied the jury (which consisted of 500 representative citizens), without any direction or summing-up from the presiding magistrate, at once gave its verdict by a majority

43

vote. If the votes were equal the case was dismissed; if the plaintiff received less than one-fifth of the total number he was fined. When the verdict was Guilty and (as in the present case) there was no penalty fixed by law, the plaintiff proposed one, the defendant another, and the jury voted between them.

The Apology *consists of three separate speeches:* (1) *Socrates' defence,* (2) *his counter-proposal for the penalty, and* (3) *a final address to the Court.*

THE APOLOGY OF SOCRATES

I DO not know what effect my accusers have had upon you, gentlemen, but for my own part I was almost carried away by them; their arguments were so convincing. On the other hand, scarcely a word of what they said was true. I was especially astonished at one of their many misrepresentations: I mean when they told you that you must be careful not to let me deceive you – the implication being that I am a skilful speaker. I thought that it was peculiarly brazen of them to tell you this without a blush, since they must know that they will soon be effectively confuted, when it becomes obvious that I have not the slightest skill as a speaker – unless, of course, by a skilful speaker they mean one who speaks the truth. If that is what they mean, I would agree that I am an orator, though not after their pattern.

My accusers, then, as I maintain, have said little or nothing that is true, but from me you shall hear the whole truth; not, I can assure you, gentlemen, in flowery language like theirs, decked out with fine words and phrases; no, what you will hear will be a straightforward speech in the first words that occur to me, confident as I am in the justice of my cause; and I do not want any of you to expect anything different. It would hardly be suitable, gentlemen, for a man of my age to address you in the artificial language of a schoolboy orator. One thing, however, I do most earnestly beg and entreat of you: if you hear me defending myself in the same language which it has been my habit to use, both in the open spaces of this city[1] (where many of you have heard me) and elsewhere, do not be surprised, and do not interrupt. Let me remind you of my position. This is my first appearance in a court of law, at the age of seventy; and so I am a complete stranger to the language of this place. Now if I were really from another country, you would naturally excuse me if I spoke in the manner and dialect in which I had been brought up; and so in the present case I make this request of you, which I think is only reasonable: to disregard the manner of my speech – it may be better or it may be worse – and to consider and concentrate your attention upon this one question, whether my claims are fair or not. That is the first duty of the juryman, just as it is the pleader's duty to speak the truth.

The proper course for me, gentlemen of the jury, is to deal first with the earliest charges that have been falsely brought against me, and with my earliest accusers; and then with the later ones. I make this distinction because I have already been accused in your hearing by a great many people for a great many years, though without a word of truth; and I am more afraid of those people than I am of Anytus and his colleagues,[2] although they are formidable enough. But the others are still more formidable; I mean the people who took hold of so many of you when you were children and tried to fill your minds with untrue accusations against me, saying 'There is a wise man called Socrates who has theories about the heavens and has investigated everything below the earth, and can make the weaker argument defeat the stronger.' It is these people, gentlemen, the disseminators of these rumours, who are my dangerous accusers; because those who hear them suppose that anyone who inquires into such matters must be an atheist. Besides, there are a great many of these accusers, and they have been accusing me now for a great many years; and what is more, they approached you at the most impressionable age, when some of you were children or adolescents; and they literally won their case by default, because there was no one to defend me. And the most fantastic thing of all is that it is impossible for me even to know and tell you their names, unless one of them happens to be a playwright.[3] All these people, who have tried to set you against me out of envy and love of slander – and some too merely passing on what they have been told by others – all these are very difficult to deal with. It is impossible to bring

them here for cross-examination; one simply has to conduct one's defence and argue one's case against an invisible
opponent, because there is no one to answer. So I ask you
to accept my statement that my critics fall into two classes:
on the one hand my immediate accusers, and on the other
those earlier ones whom I have mentioned; and you must
suppose that I have first to defend myself against the latter.
After all, you heard them abusing me longer ago and much
more violently than these more recent accusers.

Very well, then; I must begin my defence, gentlemen, and
I must try, in the short time that I have, to rid your minds
of a false impression which is the work of many years. I
should like this to be the result, gentlemen, assuming it to
be for your advantage and my own; and I should like to
be successful in my defence; but I think that it will be difficult, and I am quite aware of the nature of my task. However, let that turn out as God wills; I must obey the law
and make my defence.

Let us go back to the beginning and consider what the
charge is that has made me so unpopular, and has encouraged Meletus to draw up this indictment. Very well; what
did my critics say in attacking my character? I must read
out their affidavit, so to speak, as though they were my
legal accusers. 'Socrates is guilty of criminal meddling, in
that he inquires into things below the earth and in the sky,
and makes the weaker argument defeat the stronger, and
teaches others to follow his example.' It runs something
like that. You have seen it for yourselves in the play by
Aristophanes, where Socrates goes whirling round,[4] proclaiming that he is walking on air, and uttering a great deal
of other nonsense about things of which I know nothing
whatsoever. I mean no disrespect for such knowledge, if
anyone really is versed in it – I do not want any more law-
suits brought against me by Meletus – but the fact is, gentlemen, that I take no interest in it. What is more, I call upon
the greater part of you as witnesses to my statement, and
I appeal to all of you who have ever listened to me talking

47

(and there are a great many to whom this applies) to clear your neighbours' minds on this point. Tell one another whether any one of you has ever heard me discuss such questions briefly or at length; and then you will realize that the other popular reports about me are equally unreliable.

The fact is that there is nothing in any of these charges; and if you have heard anyone say that I try to educate people and charge a fee, there is no truth in that either. I wish that there were, because I think that it is a fine thing if a man is qualified to teach, as in the case of Gorgias of Leontini [5] and Prodicus of Ceos [6] and Hippias of Elis. [7] Each one of these is perfectly capable of going into any city and actually persuading the young men to leave the company of their fellow-citizens, with any of whom they can associate for nothing, and attach themselves to him, and pay money for the privilege, and be grateful into the bargain. There is another expert too from Paros who I discovered was here on a visit. I happened to meet a man who has paid more in sophists' fees than all the rest put together – I mean Callias [8] the son of Hipponicus; so I asked him (he has two sons, you see): 'Callias,' I said, 'if your sons had been colts or calves, we should have had no difficulty in finding and engaging a trainer to perfect their natural qualities; and this trainer would have been some sort of horse-dealer or agriculturalist. But seeing that they are human beings, whom do you intend to get as their instructor? who is the expert in perfecting the human and social qualities? I assume from the fact of your having sons that you must have considered the question. Is there such a person or not?' 'Certainly', said he. 'Who is he, and where does he come from?' said I, 'and what does he charge?' 'Evenus of Paros,[9] Socrates,' said he, 'and his fee is twenty guineas.' I felt that Evenus was to be congratulated if he really was a master of this art and taught it at such a moderate fee. I should certainly plume myself and give myself airs if I understood these things; but in fact, gentlemen, I do not.

Here perhaps one of you might interrupt me and say 'But

what is it that you do, Socrates? How is it that you have been misrepresented like this? Surely all this talk and gossip about you would never have arisen if you had confined yourself to ordinary activities, but only if your behaviour was abnormal. Tell us the explanation, if you do not want us to invent it for ourselves.' This seems to me to be a reasonable request, and I will try to explain to you what it is that has given me this false notoriety; so please give me your attention. Perhaps some of you will think that I am not being serious; but I assure you that I am going to tell you the whole truth.

I have gained this reputation, gentlemen, from nothing more or less than a kind of wisdom. What kind of wisdom do I mean? Human wisdom, I suppose. It seems that I really am wise in this limited sense. Presumably the geniuses whom I mentioned just now are wise in a wisdom that is more than human; I do not know how else to account for it. I certainly have no knowledge of such wisdom, and anyone who says that I have is a liar and wilful slanderer. Now, gentlemen, please do not interrupt me if I seem to make an extravagant claim; for what I am going to tell you is not my own opinion; I am going to refer you to an unimpeachable authority. I shall call as witness to my wisdom (such as it is) the god at Delphi.[10]

You know Chaerephon,[11] of course. He was a friend of mine from boyhood, and a good democrat who played his part with the rest of you in the recent expulsion [12] and restoration. And you know what he was like; how enthusiastic he was over anything that he had once undertaken. Well, one day he actually went to Delphi and asked this question of the god – as I said before, gentlemen, please do not interrupt – he asked whether there was anyone wiser than myself. The priestess replied that there was no one. As Chaerephon is dead, the evidence for my statement will be supplied by his brother,[13] who is here in court.

Please consider my object in telling you this. I want to explain to you how the attack upon my reputation first

49

started. When I heard about the oracle's answer, I said to
myself 'What does the god mean? Why does he not use
plain language? I am only too conscious that I have no
claim to wisdom, great or small; so what can he mean by
asserting that I am the wisest man in the world? He cannot
be telling a lie; that would not be right for him.'

After puzzling about it for some time, I set myself at last
with considerable reluctance to check the truth of it in the
following way. I went to interview a man with a high reputation for wisdom, because I felt that here if anywhere I
should succeed in disproving the oracle and pointing out
to my divine authority 'You said that I was the wisest of
men, but here is a man who is wiser than I am.'

Well, I gave a thorough examination to this person – I
need not mention his name, but it was one of our politicians that I was studying when I had this experience – and
in conversation with him I formed the impression that
although in many people's opinion, and especially in his
own, he appeared to be wise, in fact he was not. Then when
I began to try to show him that he only thought he was
wise and was not really so, my efforts were resented both
by him and by many of the other people present. However,
I reflected as I walked away: 'Well, I am certainly wiser
than this man. It is only too likely that neither of us has
any knowledge to boast of; but he thinks that he knows
something which he does not know, whereas I am quite
conscious of my ignorance. At any rate it seems that I am
wiser than he is to this small extent, that I do not think that
I know what I do not know.'

After this I went on to interview a man with an even
greater reputation for wisdom, and I formed the same
impression again; and here too I incurred the resentment
of the man himself and a number of others.

From that time on I interviewed one person after another. I realized with distress and alarm that I was making
myself unpopular, but I felt compelled to put my religious
duty first; since I was trying to find out the meaning of the

oracle, I was bound to interview everyone who had a reputation for knowledge. And by Dog,[14] gentlemen! (for I must be frank with you) my honest impression was this: it seemed to me, as I pursued my investigation at the god's command, that the people with the greatest reputations were almost entirely deficient, while others who were supposed to be their inferiors were much better qualified in practical intelligence.

I want you to think of my adventures as a sort of pilgrimage [15] undertaken to establish the truth of the oracle once for all. After I had finished with the politicians I turned to the poets, dramatic, lyric, and all the rest, in the belief that here I should expose myself as a comparative ignoramus. I used to pick up what I thought were some of their most perfect works and question them closely about the meaning of what they had written, in the hope of incidentally enlarging my own knowledge. Well, gentlemen, I hesitate to tell you the truth, but it must be told. It is hardly an exaggeration to say that any of the bystanders could have explained those poems better than their actual authors. So I soon made up my mind about the poets too: I decided that it was not wisdom that enabled them to write their poetry, but a kind of instinct or inspiration, such as you find in seers and prophets who deliver all their sublime messages without knowing in the least what they mean. It seemed clear to me that the poets were in much the same case; and I also observed that the very fact that they were poets made them think that they had a perfect understanding of all other subjects, of which they were totally ignorant. So I left that line of inquiry too with the same sense of advantage that I had felt in the case of the politicians.

Last of all I turned to the skilled craftsmen. I knew quite well that I had practically no technical qualifications myself, and I was sure that I should find them full of impressive knowledge. In this I was not disappointed; they understood things which I did not, and to that extent they were wiser than I was. But, gentlemen, these professional experts seemed to share the same failing which I had noticed in the poets; I mean that on the strength of their technical proficiency they claimed a perfect understanding of every other subject, however important; and I felt that this error more than outweighed their positive wisdom. So I made myself spokesman for the oracle, and asked myself whether I would rather be as I was – neither wise with their wisdom nor stupid with their stupidity – or possess both qualities as they did. I replied through myself to the oracle that it was best for me to be as I was.

The effect of these investigations of mine, gentlemen, has been to arouse against me a great deal of hostility, and hostility of a particularly bitter and persistent kind, which has resulted in various malicious suggestions, including the description of me as a professor of wisdom. This is due to the fact that whenever I succeed in disproving another person's claim to wisdom in a given subject, the bystanders assume that I know everything about that subject myself. But the truth of the matter, gentlemen, is pretty certainly this: that real wisdom is the property of God, and this oracle is his way of telling us that human wisdom has little or no value. It seems to me that he is not referring literally to Socrates, but has merely taken my name as an example, as if he would say to us 'The wisest of you men is he who has realized, like Socrates, that in respect of wisdom he is really worthless.'

That is why I still go about seeking and searching in obedience to the divine command, if I think that anyone is wise, whether citizen or stranger; and when I think that any person is not wise, I try to help the cause of God by proving that he is not. This occupation has kept me too busy to do much either in politics or in my own affairs; in fact, my service to God has reduced me to extreme poverty.

There is another reason for my being unpopular. A number of young men with wealthy fathers and plenty of leisure have deliberately attached themselves to me because they enjoy hearing other people cross-questioned. These often take me as their model, and go on to try to question other persons; whereupon, I suppose, they find an unlimited number of people who think that they know something, but really know little or nothing. Consequently their victims become annoyed, not with themselves but with me; and they complain that there is a pestilential busybody called Socrates who fills young people's heads with wrong ideas. If you ask them what he does, and what he teaches that has this effect, they have no answer, not knowing what to say; but as they do not want to admit their confusion, they fall back on the stock charges against any philosopher: that he teaches his pupils about things in the heavens and below the earth, and to disbelieve in gods, and to make the weaker argument defeat the stronger. They would be very loath, I fancy, to admit the truth: which is that they are being convicted of pretending to knowledge when they are entirely ignorant. So, jealous, I suppose, for their own reputation, and also energetic and numerically strong, and provided with a plausible and carefully worked out case against me, these people have been dinning into your ears for a long time past their violent denunciations of myself. There you have the causes which led to the attack upon me by Meletus and Anytus and Lycon, Meletus being aggrieved on behalf of the poets, Anytus on behalf of the professional men and politicians, and Lycon on behalf of the orators. So, as I said at the beginning, I should be surprised if I were able, in the short time that I have, to rid your minds of a misconception so deeply implanted.

There, gentlemen, you have the true facts, which I present to you without any concealment or suppression, great or small. I am fairly certain that this plain speaking of mine is the cause of my unpopularity; and this really goes to prove that my statements are true, and that I have described correctly the nature and the grounds of the calumny which has been brought against me. Whether you inquire into them now or later, you will find the facts as I have just described them.

So much for my defence against the charges brought by the first group of my accusers. I shall now try to defend myself against Meletus – high-principled and patriotic as he claims to be – and after that against the rest.

Let us first consider their deposition again, as though it represented a fresh prosecution. It runs something like this: 'Socrates is guilty of corrupting the minds of the young, and of believing in deities of his own invention instead of the gods recognized by the State.' Such is the charge; let us examine its points one by one.

First it says that I am guilty of corrupting the young. But I say, gentlemen, that Meletus is guilty of treating a serious matter with levity, since he summons people to stand their trial on frivolous grounds, and professes concern and keen anxiety in matters about which he has never had the slightest interest. I will try to prove this to your satisfaction.

Come now, Meletus, tell me this. You regard it as supremely important, do you not, that our young people should be exposed to the best possible influence? 'I do.' Very well, then; tell these gentlemen who it is that influences the young for the better. Obviously you must know, if you are so much interested. You have discovered the vicious influence, as you say, in myself, and you are now prosecuting me before these gentlemen; speak up and inform them who it is that has a good influence upon the young. – You see, Meletus, that you are tongue-tied and cannot answer. Do you not feel that this is discreditable, and a sufficient proof in itself of what I said, that you have no interest in the subject? Tell me, my friend, who is it that makes the young good? 'The laws.' That is not what I mean, my dear sir; I am asking you to name the *person* whose first business it is to know the laws. 'These gentlemen here, Socrates, the members of the jury.' Do you mean, Meletus, that they have the ability to educate the young, and to make them better? 'Certainly.' Does this apply to all jurymen, or only to some? 'To all of them.' Excellent! a generous sup-

ply of benefactors. Well, then, do these spectators who are
present in court have an improving influence, or not? 'Yes,
they do.' And what about the members of the Council?
'Yes, the Councillors too.' But surely, Meletus, the members of the Assembly [16] do not corrupt the young? Or do
all of them too exert an improving influence? 'Yes, they
do.' Then it would seem that the whole population of
Athens has a refining effect upon the young, except myself;
and I alone demoralize them. Is that your meaning? 'Most
emphatically, yes.' This is certainly a most unfortunate
quality that you have detected in me. Well, let me put another question to you. Take the case of horses; do you
believe that those who improve them make up the whole
of mankind, and that there is only one person who has a
bad effect on them? Or is the truth just the opposite, that
the ability to improve them belongs to one person or to
very few persons, who are horse-trainers, whereas most
people, if they have to do with horses and make use of them,
do them harm? Is not this the case, Meletus, both with
horses and with all other animals? Of course it is, whether
you and Anytus deny it or not. It would be a singular
dispensation of fortune for our young people if there is
only one person who corrupts them, while all the rest have
a beneficial effect. But I need say no more; there is ample
proof, Meletus, that you have never bothered your head
about the young; and you make it perfectly clear that you
have never taken the slightest interest in the cause for the
sake of which you are now indicting me.

Here is another point. Tell me seriously, Meletus, is it
better to live in a good or in a bad community? Answer my
question, like a good fellow; there is nothing difficult about
it. Is it not true that wicked people have a bad effect upon
those with whom they are in the closest contact, and that
good people have a good effect? 'Quite true.' Is there anyone who prefers to be harmed rather than benefited by his
associates? Answer me, my good man; the law commands
you to answer. Is there anyone who prefers to be harmed?

'Of course not.' Well, then, when you summon me before this court for corrupting the young and making their characters worse, do you mean that I do so intentionally or unintentionally? 'I mean intentionally.' Why, Meletus, are you at your age so much wiser than I at mine? You have discovered that bad people always have a bad effect, and good people a good effect, upon their nearest neighbours; am I so hopelessly ignorant as not even to realize that by spoiling the character of one of my companions I shall run the risk of getting some harm from him? because nothing else would make me commit this grave offence intentionally. No, I do not believe it, Meletus, and I do not suppose that anyone else does. Either I have not a bad influence, or it is unintentional; so that in either case your accusation is false. And if I unintentionally have a bad influence, the correct procedure in cases of such involuntary misdemeanours is not to summon the culprit before this court, but to take him aside privately for instruction and reproof; because obviously if my eyes are opened, I shall stop doing what I do not intend to do. But you deliberately avoided my company in the past and refused to enlighten me, and now you bring me before this court, which is the place appointed for those who need punishment, not for those who need enlightenment.

It is quite clear by now, gentlemen, that Meletus, as I said before, has never shown any degree of interest in this subject. However, I invite you to tell us, Meletus, in what sense you make out that I corrupt the minds of the young. Surely the terms of your indictment make it clear that you accuse me of teaching them to believe in new deities instead of the gods recognized by the State; is not that the teaching of mine which you say has this demoralizing effect? 'That is precisely what I maintain.' Then I appeal to you, Meletus, in the name of these same gods about whom we are speaking, to explain yourself a little more clearly to myself and to the jury, because I cannot make out what your point is. Is it that I teach people to believe in some gods (which implies that I myself believe in gods, and am not a complete atheist, so that I am not guilty on that score), but in different gods from those recognized by the State, so that your accusation rests upon the fact that they are different? Or do you assert that I believe in no gods at all, and teach others to do the same? 'Yes; I say that you disbelieve in gods altogether.' You surprise me, Meletus; what is your object in saying that? Do you suggest that I do not believe that the sun and moon are gods,[17] as is the general belief of all mankind? 'He certainly does not, gentlemen of the jury, since he says that the sun is a stone and the moon a mass of earth.' Do you imagine that you are prosecuting Anaxagoras, my dear Meletus? Have you so poor an opinion of these gentlemen, and do you assume them to be so illiterate as not to know that the writings of Anaxagoras of Clazomenae [18] are full of theories like these? and do you seriously suggest that it is from me that the young get these ideas, when they can buy them on occasion in the market-place [19] for a shilling at most, and so have the laugh on Socrates if he claims them for his own, to say nothing of their being so silly? Tell me honestly, Meletus, is that your opinion of me? do I believe in no god? 'No, none at all; not in the slightest degree.' You are not at all convincing, Meletus; not even to yourself, I suspect. In my opinion, gentlemen, this man is a thoroughly selfish bully, and has brought this action against me out of sheer wanton aggressiveness and self-assertion. He seems to be devising a sort of intelligence test for me, saying to himself 'Will the infallible Socrates realize that I am contradicting myself for my own amusement, or shall I succeed in deceiving him and the rest of my audience?' It certainly seems to me that he is contradicting himself in this indictment, which might just as well run 'Socrates is guilty of not believing in the gods, but believing in the gods'. And this is pure flippancy.

I ask you to examine with me, gentlemen, the line of reasoning which leads me to this conclusion. You, Meletus, will oblige us by answering my questions. Will you all kindly remember, as I requested at the beginning, not to interrupt if I conduct the discussion in my customary way?

Is there anyone in the world, Meletus, who believes in human activities, and not in human beings? Make him answer, gentlemen, and don't let him keep on making these continual objections. Is there anyone who does not believe in horses, but believes in horses' activities? or who does not believe in musicians, but believes in musical activities? No, there is not, my worthy friend. If you do not want to answer, I will supply it for you and for these gentlemen too. But the next question you must answer: Is there anyone who believes in supernatural activities and not in supernatural beings? [20] 'No.' How good of you to give a bare answer under compulsion by the court! Well, do you assert that I believe and teach others to believe in supernatural activities? It does not matter whether they are new or old; the fact remains that I believe in them according to your statement; indeed you solemnly swore as much in your affidavit. But if I believe in supernatural activities, it follows inevitably that I also believe in supernatural beings. Is not that so? It is; I assume your assent, since you do not answer. Do we not hold that supernatural beings are either gods or the children of gods? Do you agree or not? 'Certainly.' Then if I believe in supernatural beings, as you assert, if these supernatural beings are gods in any sense, we shall reach the conclusion which I mentioned just now when I said that you were testing my intelligence for your own amusement, by stating first that I do not believe in gods, and then again that I do, since I believe in supernatural beings. If on the other hand these supernatural beings are bastard children [21] of the gods by nymphs or other mothers, as they are reputed to be, who in the world would believe in the children of gods and not in the gods themselves? It would be as ridiculous as to believe in the young of horses or donkeys and not in horses and donkeys themselves. No, Meletus; there is no avoiding the conclusion that you brought this charge against me as a test of my wisdom, or else in despair of finding a genuine offence of which to accuse me. As for your prospect of convincing any living person with even a smattering of intelligence that belief in supernatural and divine activities does not imply belief in supernatural and divine beings, and *vice versa*, it is outside all the bounds of possibility.

As a matter of fact, gentlemen, I do not feel that it requires much defence to clear myself of Meletus' accusation; what I have said already is enough. But you know very well the truth of what I said in an earlier part of my speech, that I have incurred a great deal of bitter hostility; and this is what will bring about my destruction, if anything does; not Meletus nor Anytus, but the slander and jealousy of a very large section of the people. They have been fatal to a great many other innocent men, and I suppose will continue to be so; there is no likelihood that they will stop at me. But perhaps someone will say 'Do you feel no compunction, Socrates, at having followed a line of action which puts you in danger of the death-penalty?' I might fairly reply to him 'You are mistaken, my friend, if you think that a man who is worth anything ought to spend his time weighing up the prospects of life and death. He has only one thing to consider in performing any action; that is, whether he is acting rightly or wrongly, like a good man or a bad one. On your view the heroes who died at Troy would be poor creatures, especially the son of Thetis.[22] He, if you remember, made so light of danger in comparison with incurring dishonour that when his goddess mother warned him, eager as he was to kill Hector, in some such words as these, I fancy, "My son, if you avenge your comrade Patroclus' death and kill Hector, you will die yourself;

> Next after Hector is thy fate prepared,"

– when he heard this warning, he made light of his death and danger, being much more afraid of an ignoble life and of failing to avenge his friends. "Let me die forthwith," said he, "when I have requited the villain, rather than remain here by the beaked ships to be mocked, a burden on the ground." Do you suppose that he gave a thought to death and danger?'

The truth of the matter is this, gentlemen. Where a man has once taken up his stand, either because it seems best to him or in obedience to his orders, there I believe he is bound to remain and face the danger, taking no account of death or anything else before dishonour.

This being so, it would be shocking inconsistency on my part, gentlemen, if, when the officers whom you chose to command me assigned me my position at Potidaea [23] and Amphipolis [24] and Delium, [25] I remained at my post like anyone else and faced death, and yet afterwards, when God appointed me, as I supposed and believed, to the duty of leading the philosophic life, examining myself and others, I were then through fear of death or of any other danger to desert my post. That would indeed be shocking, and then I might really with justice be summoned into court for not believing in the gods, and disobeying the oracle, and being afraid of death, and thinking that I am wise when I am not. For let me tell you, gentlemen, that to be afraid of death is only another form of thinking that one is wise when one is not; it is to think that one knows what one does not know. No one knows with regard to death whether it is not really the greatest blessing that can happen to a man; but people dread it as though they were certain that it is the greatest evil; and this ignorance, which thinks that it knows what it does not, must surely be ignorance most culpable. This, I take it, gentlemen, is the degree, and this the nature of my advantage over the rest of mankind; and if I were to claim to be wiser than my neighbour in any respect, it would be in this: that not possessing any real knowledge of what comes after death, I am also conscious that I do not possess it. But I do know that to do wrong and to disobey my superior, whether God or man, is wicked and dishonourable; and so I shall never feel more fear or aversion for something which, for all I know, may really be a blessing, than for those evils which I know to be evils.

Suppose, then, that you acquit me, and pay no attention to Anytus, who has said that either I should not have appeared before this court at all, or, since I have appeared here, I must be put to death, because if I once escaped your sons would all immediately become utterly demoralized by putting the teaching of Socrates into practice. Suppose that, in view of this, you said to me 'Socrates, on this occasion we shall disregard Anytus and acquit you, but only on one condition, that you give up spending your time on this quest and stop philosophizing. If we catch you going on in the same way, you shall be put to death.' Well, supposing, as I said, that you should offer to acquit me on these terms, I should reply 'Gentlemen, I am your very grateful and devoted servant, but I owe a greater obedience to God than to you; and so long as I draw breath and have my faculties, I shall never stop practising philosophy and exhorting you and elucidating the truth for everyone that I meet. I shall go on saying, in my usual way, "My very good friend, you are an Athenian and belong to a city which is the greatest and most famous in the world for its wisdom and strength. Are you not ashamed that you give your attention to acquiring as much money as possible, and similarly with reputation and honour, and give no attention or thought to truth and understanding and the perfection of your soul?" And if any of you disputes this and professes to care about these things, I shall not at once let him go or leave him; no, I shall question him and examine him and test him; and if it appears that in spite of his profession he has made no real progress towards goodness, I shall reprove him for neglecting what is of supreme importance, and giving his attention to trivialities. I shall do this to everyone that I meet, young or old, foreigner or fellow citizen; but especially to you my fellow-citizens, inasmuch as you are closer to me in kinship. This, I do assure you, is what my God commands; and it is my belief that no greater good has ever befallen you in this city than my service to my God; for I spend all my time going about trying to persuade you, young and old, to make your first and chief concern not for your bodies nor for your possessions, but for the highest welfare of your souls, proclaiming as I go 'Wealth does not bring goodness, but goodness brings wealth and every other blessing, both to the individual and to the State.' Now if I corrupt the young by this message, the message would seem to be harmful; but if anyone says that my message is different from this, he is talking nonsense. And so, gentlemen, I would say, 'You can please yourselves whether you listen to Anytus or not, and whether you acquit me or not; you know that I am not going to alter my conduct, not even if I have to die a hundred deaths.'

Order, please, gentlemen! Remember my request to give me a hearing without interruption; besides, I believe that it will be to your advantage to listen. I am going to tell you something else, which may provoke a storm of protest; but please restrain yourselves. I assure you that if I am what I claim to be, and you put me to death, you will harm yourselves more than me. Neither Meletus nor Anytus can do me any harm at all; they would not have the power, because I do not believe that the law of God permits a better man to be harmed by a worse. No doubt my accuser might put me to death or have me banished or deprived of civic rights; but even if he thinks, as he probably does (and others too, I dare say), that these are great calamities, I do not think so; I believe that it is far worse to do what he is doing now, trying to put an innocent man to death. For this reason, gentlemen, so far from pleading on my own behalf, as might be supposed, I am really pleading on yours, to save you from misusing the gift of God by condemning me. If you put me to death, you will not easily find anyone to take my place. It is literally true (even if it sounds rather comical) that God has specially appointed me to this city, as though it were a large thoroughbred horse which because of its great size is inclined to be lazy and needs the stimulation of some stinging fly. It seems to me that God has attached me to this city to perform the office of such a fly; and all day long I never cease to settle here, there, and everywhere, rousing, persuading, reproving every one of you. You will not easily find another like me, gentlemen, and if you take my advice you will spare my life. I suspect, however, that before long you will awake from your drowsing, and in your annoyance you will take Anytus' advice and finish me off with a single slap; and then you will go on sleeping till the end of your days, unless God in his care for you sends someone to take my place.

If you doubt whether I am really the sort of person who would have been sent to this city as a gift from God, you can convince yourselves by looking at it in this way. Does it seem natural that I should have neglected my own affairs and endured the humiliation of allowing my family to be neglected for all these years, while I busied myself all the time on your behalf, going like a father or an elder brother to see each one of you privately, and urging you to set your thoughts on goodness? If I had got any enjoyment from it, or if I had been paid for my good advice, there would have been some explanation for my conduct; but as it is you can see for yourselves that although my accusers unblushingly charge me with all sorts of other crimes, there is one thing that they have not had the impudence to pretend on any testimony, and that is that I have ever exacted or asked a fee from anyone. The witness that I can offer to prove the truth of my statement is, I think, a convincing one – my poverty.

It may seem curious that I should go round giving advice like this and busying myself in people's private affairs, and yet never venture publicly to address you as a whole and advise on matters of state. The reason for this is what you have often heard me say before on many other occasions: that I am subject to a divine or supernatural experience, which Meletus saw fit to travesty in his indictment. It began in my early childhood – a sort of voice which comes to me; and when it comes it always dissuades me from what I am proposing to do, and never urges me on. It is this that debars me from entering public life, and a very good thing too, in my opinion; because you may be quite sure, gentlemen, that if I had tried long ago to engage in politics, I should long ago have lost my life, without doing any good either to you or to myself. Please do not be offended if I tell you the truth. No man on earth who conscientiously opposes either you or any other organized democracy, and flatly prevents a great many wrongs and illegalities from taking place in the state to which he belongs, can possibly escape with his life. The true champion of justice, if he intends to survive even for a short time, must necessarily confine himself to private life and leave politics alone.

I will offer you substantial proofs of what I have said; not theories, but what you can appreciate better, facts. Listen while I describe my actual experiences, so that you may know that I would never submit wrongly to any authority through fear of death, but would refuse even at the cost of my life. It will be a commonplace story, such as you often hear in the courts; but it is true.

The only office which I have ever held in our city, gentlemen, was when I was elected to the Council.[26] It so happened that our group was acting as the executive when you decided that the ten commanders who had failed to rescue the men who were lost in the naval engagement [27] should be tried *en bloc*; which was illegal, as you all recognized later. On this occasion I was the only member of the executive who insisted that you should not act unconstitutionally, and voted against the proposal; and although your leaders were all ready to denounce and arrest me, and you were all urging them on at the top of your voices, I thought that it was my duty to face it out on the side of law and justice rather than support you, through fear of prison or death, in your wrong decision.

This happened while we were still under a democracy. When the oligarchy came into power, the Thirty Commissioners in their turn summoned me and four others to the Round Chamber [28] and instructed us to go and fetch Leon of Salamis from his home for execution. This was of course only one of many instances in which they issued such instructions, their object being to implicate as many people as possible in their wickedness. On this occasion, however, I again made it clear not by my words but by my actions that death did not matter to me at all (if that is not too strong an expression); but that it mattered all the world to me that I should do nothing wrong or wicked. Powerful as it was, that government did not terrify me into doing a wrong action; when we came out of the Round Chamber the other four went off to Salamis and arrested Leon, and I went home. I should probably have been put to death for this, if the government had not fallen soon afterwards. There are plenty of people who will testify to these statements.

Do you suppose that I should have lived as long as I have if I had moved in the sphere of public life, and conducting myself in that sphere like an honourable man, had always upheld the cause of right, and conscientiously set this end above all other things? Not by a very long way, gentlemen; neither would any other man. You will find that throughout my life I have been consistent in any public duties that I have performed, and the same also in my personal dealings: I have never countenanced any action that was incompatible with justice on the part of any person, including those whom some people maliciously call my pupils. I have never set up as any man's teacher; but if anyone, young or old, is eager to hear me conversing and carrying out my private mission, I never grudge him the opportunity; nor do I charge a fee for talking to him, and refuse to talk without one; I am ready to answer questions for rich and poor alike, and I am equally ready if anyone prefers to listen to me and answer my questions. If any given one of these people becomes a good citizen or a bad one, I cannot fairly be held responsible, since I have never promised or imparted any teaching to anybody; and if anyone asserts that he has ever learned or heard from me privately anything which was not open to everyone else, you may be quite sure that he is not telling the truth.

But how is it that some people enjoy spending a great deal of time in my company? You have heard the reason, gentlemen; I told you quite frankly. It is because they enjoy hearing me examine those who think that they are wise when they are not; an experience which has its amusing side. This duty I have accepted, as I said, in obedience to God's commands given in oracles and dreams [29] and in every other way that any other divine dispensation has ever impressed a duty upon man. This is a true statement, gentlemen, and easy to verify. If it is a fact that I am in process of corrupting some of the young, and have succeeded already in corrupting others; and if it were a fact that some of the latter, being now grown up, had discovered that I had ever given them bad advice when they were young, surely they ought now to be coming forward to denounce and punish me; and if they did not like to do it themselves, you would expect some of their families – their fathers and brothers and other near relations – to remember it now, if their own flesh and blood had suffered any harm from me. Certainly a great many of them have found their way into this court, as I can see for myself: first Crito [30] over there, my contemporary and near neighbour, the father of this young man Critobulus; and then Lysanias of Sphettus,[31] the father of Aeschines here; and next Antiphon of Cephisia, over there, the father of Epigenes. Then besides there are all those whose brothers have been members of our circle: Nicostratus the son of Theozotides, the brother of Theodotus – but Theodotus is dead, so he cannot appeal to his brother – and Paralius here, the son of Demodocus; his brother was Theages. And here is Adimantus the son of Ariston, whose brother Plato is over there; and Aeantodorus, whose brother

Apollodorus is here on this side. I can name many more besides, some of whom Meletus most certainly ought to have produced as witness in the course of his speech. If he forgot to do so then, let him do it now – I am willing to make way for him; let him state whether he has any such evidence to offer. On the contrary, gentlemen, you will find that they are all prepared to help me – the corrupter and evil genius of their nearest and dearest relatives, as Meletus and Anytus say. The actual victims of my corrupting influence might perhaps be excused for helping me; but as for the uncorrupted, their relations of mature age, what other reason can they have for helping me except the right and proper one, that they know Meletus is lying and I am telling the truth?

There, gentlemen: that, and perhaps a little more to the same effect, is the substance of what I can say in my defence. It may be that some one of you, remembering his own case, will be annoyed that whereas he, in standing his trial upon a less serious charge than this, made pitiful appeals to the jury with floods of tears, and had his infant children produced in court to excite the maximum of sympathy, and many of his relatives and friends as well, I on the contrary intend to do nothing of the sort, and that although I am facing (as it might appear) the utmost danger. It may be that one of you, reflecting on these facts, will be prejudiced against me, and being irritated by his reflections, will give his vote in anger. If one of you is so disposed – I do not expect it, but there is the possibility – I think that I should be quite justified in saying to him 'My dear sir, of course I have some relatives. To quote the very words of Homer, even I am not sprung "from an oak or from a rock",[32] but from human parents, and consequently I have relatives; yes, and sons [33] too, gentlemen, three of them, one almost grown up and the other two only children; but all the same I am not going to produce them here and beseech you to acquit me.'

67

Why do I not intend to do anything of this kind? Not out of perversity, gentlemen, nor out of contempt for you; whether I am brave or not in the face of death has nothing to do with it; the point is that for my own credit and yours and for the credit of the state as a whole, I do not think that it is right for me to use any of these methods at my age and with my reputation – which may be true or it may be false, but at any rate the view is held that Socrates is different from the common run of mankind. Now if those of you who are supposed to be distinguished for wisdom or courage or any other virtue are to behave in this way, it would be a disgrace. I have often noticed that some people of this type, for all their high standing, go to extraordinary lengths when they come up for trial, which shows that they think it will be a dreadful thing to lose their lives; as though they would be immortal if you did not put them to death! In my opinion these people bring disgrace upon our city. Any of our visitors might be excused for thinking that the finest specimens of Athenian manhood, whom their fellow-citizens select on their merits to rule over them and hold other high positions, are no better than women. If you have even the smallest reputation, gentlemen, you ought not to descend to these methods; and if we do so, you must not give us licence. On the contrary, you must make it clear that anyone who stages these pathetic scenes and so brings ridicule upon our city is far more likely to be condemned than if he kept perfectly quiet.

But apart from all question of appearances, gentlemen, I do not think that it is right for a man to appeal to the jury or to get himself acquitted by doing so; he ought to inform them of the facts and convince them by argument. The jury does not sit to dispense justice as a favour, but to decide where justice lies; and the oath which they have sworn is not to show favour at their own discretion, but to return a just and lawful verdict. It follows that we must not develop in you, nor you allow to grow in yourselves, the habit of perjury; that would be sinful for us both. Therefore you must not expect me, gentlemen, to behave towards you in a way which I consider neither reputable nor moral nor consistent with my religious duty; and above all you must not expect it when I stand charged with impiety by Meletus here. Surely it is obvious that if I tried to persuade you and prevail upon you by my entreaties to go against your solemn oath, I should be teaching you contempt for religion; and by my very defence I should be accusing myself of having no religious belief. But that is very far from the truth. I have a more sincere belief, gentlemen, than any of my accusers; and I leave it to you and to God to judge me as it shall be best for me and for yourselves.

(The verdict is 'Guilty', and Meletus proposes the penalty of death)

There are a great many reasons, gentlemen, why I am not distressed by this result – I mean your condemnation of me – but the chief reason is that the result was not unexpected. What does surprise me is the number of votes cast on the two sides. I should never have believed that it would be such a close thing; but now it seems that if a mere thirty votes [34] had gone the other way, I should have been acquitted. Even as it is, I feel that so far as Meletus' part is concerned I have been acquitted; and not only that, but anyone can see that if Anytus and Lycon had not come forward to accuse me, Meletus would actually have forfeited his £50 for not having obtained one-fifth [35] of the votes.

However, we must face the fact that he demands the death-penalty. Very good. What alternative penalty shall I propose to you, gentlemen? Obviously it must be adequate. Well, what penalty do I deserve to pay or suffer, in view of what I have done?

I have never lived an ordinary quiet life. I did not care for the things that most people care about: making money, having a comfortable home, high military or civil rank, and all the other activities – political appointments, secret societies, party organizations – which go on in our city; I thought that I was really too strict in my principles to survive if I went in for this sort of thing. So instead of taking a course which would have done no good either to you or to me, I set myself to do you individually in private what I hold to be the greatest possible service: I tried to persuade each one of you not to think more of practical advantages than of his mental and moral well-being, or in general to think more of advantage than of well-being in the case of the state or of anything else. What do I deserve for behaving in this way? Some reward, gentlemen, if I am bound to suggest what I really deserve; and what is more, a reward which would be appropriate for myself. Well, what is appropriate for a poor man who is a public benefactor and who requires leisure for giving you moral encouragement? Nothing could be more appropriate for such a person than free maintenance [36] at the State's expense. He deserves it much more than any victor in the races at Olympia, whether he wins with a single horse or a pair or a team of four. These people give you the semblance of success, but I give you the reality; they do not need maintenance, but I do. So if I am to suggest an appropriate penalty which is strictly in accordance with justice, I suggest free maintenance by the State.

Perhaps when I say this I may give you the impression, as I did in my remarks about exciting sympathy and making passionate appeals, that I am showing a deliberate perversity. That is not so, gentlemen; the real position is this. I am convinced that I never wrong anyone intentionally, but I cannot convince you of this, because we have had so little time for discussion. If it was your practice, as it is with other nations, to give not one day but several to the hearing of capital trials, I believe that you might have been convinced; but under present conditions it is not easy to dispose of grave allegations in a short space of time. So being convinced that I do no wrong to anybody, I can hardly be expected to wrong myself by asserting that I deserve something bad, or by proposing a corresponding penalty. Why should I? For fear of suffering this penalty proposed by Meletus, when, as I said, I do not know whether it is a good thing or a bad? Do you expect me to choose something which I know very well is bad by making my counter-proposal? Imprisonment? Why should I spend my days in prison, in subjection to the periodically appointed officers of the law? A fine, with imprisonment until it is paid? In my case the effect would be just the same, because I have no money to pay a fine. Or shall I suggest banishment? [37] You would very likely accept the suggestion.

I should have to be desperately in love with life to do that, gentlemen. I am not so blind that I cannot see that you, my fellow-citizens, have come to the end of your patience with my discussions and conversations; you have found them too irksome and irritating, and now you are trying to get rid of them. Will any other people find them easy to put up with? That is most unlikely, gentlemen. A fine life I should have if I left this country at my age and spent the rest of my days trying one city after another and being turned out every time! I know very well that wherever I go the young people will listen to my conversation just as they do here; and if I try to keep them off, they will make their elders drive me out, while if I do not, the fathers and other relatives will drive me out of their own accord for the sake of the young.

Perhaps someone may say 'But surely, Socrates, after you have left us you can spend the rest of your life in quietly minding your own business.' This is the hardest thing of all to make some of you understand. If I say that this would be disobedience to God, and that is why I cannot 'mind my own business', you will not believe that I am serious. If on the other hand I tell you that to let no day pass without discussing goodness and all the other subjects about which you hear me talking and examining both myself and others is really the very best thing that a man can do, and that life without this sort of examination is not worth living, you will be even less inclined to believe me. Nevertheless that is how it is, gentlemen, as I maintain; though it is not easy to convince you of it. Besides, I am not accustomed to think of myself as deserving punishment. If I had money, I would have suggested a fine that I could afford, because that would not have done me any harm. As it is, I cannot, because I have none; unless of course you like to fix the penalty at what I could pay. I suppose I could probably afford five pounds [38]. I suggest a fine of that amount.

One moment, gentlemen. Plato here, and Crito and Critobulus and Apollodorus, want me to propose £150, on their security. Very well, I agree to this sum, and you can rely upon these gentlemen for its payment.

(The jury decides for the death-penalty)

Well, gentlemen, for the sake of a very small gain in time you are going to earn the reputation – and the blame from those who wish to disparage our city – of having put Socrates to death, 'that wise man' – because they will say I am wise even if I am not, these people who want to find fault with you. If you had waited just a little while, you would have had your way in the course of nature. You can see that I am well on in life and near to death. I am saying this not to all of you but to those who voted for my execution, [39] and I have something else to say to them as well.

No doubt you think, gentlemen, that I have been condemned for lack of the arguments which I could have used if I had thought it right to leave nothing unsaid or undone to secure my acquittal. But that is very far from the truth. It is not a lack of arguments that has caused my condemnation, but a lack of effrontery and impudence, and the fact that I have refused to address you in the way which would give you most pleasure. You would have liked to hear me weep and wail, doing and saying all sorts of things which I regard as unworthy of myself, but which you are used to hearing from other people. But I did not think then that I ought to stoop to servility because I was in danger, and I do not regret now the way in which I pleaded my case; I would much rather die as the result of this defence than live as the result of the other sort. In a court of law, just as in warfare, neither I nor any other ought to use his wits to escape death by any means. In battle it is often obvious that you could escape being killed by giving up your arms and throwing yourself upon the mercy of your pursuers; and in every kind of danger there are plenty of devices for avoiding death if you are unscrupulous enough to stick at nothing. But I suggest, gentlemen, that the difficulty is not so much to escape death; the real difficulty is to escape from doing wrong, which is far more fleet of foot. In this present instance I, the slow old man, have been overtaken by the slower of the two, but my accusers, who are clever and quick, have been overtaken by the faster: by iniquity. When I leave this court I shall go away condemned by you to death, but they will go away convicted by Truth herself of depravity and wickedness. And they accept their sentence even as I accept mine. No doubt it was bound to be so, and I think that the result is fair enough.

Having said so much, I feel moved to prophesy to you who have given your vote against me; for I am now at that point where the gift of prophecy comes most readily to men: at the point of death. I tell you, my executioners, that as soon as I am dead, vengeance shall fall upon you with a punishment far more painful than your killing of me. You have brought about my death in the belief that through it you will be delivered from submitting your conduct to criticism; but I say that the result will be just the opposite. You will have more critics, whom up till now I have restrained without your knowing it; and being younger they will be harsher to you and will cause you more annoyance.

If you expect to stop denunciation of your wrong way of life by putting people to death, there is something amiss with your reasoning. This way of escape is neither possible nor creditable; the best and easiest way is not to stop the mouths of others, but to make yourselves as good men as you can. This is my last message to you who voted for my condemnation.

As for you who voted for my acquittal, I should very much like to say a few words to reconcile you to the result, while the officials are busy and I am not yet on my way to the place where I must die. I ask you, gentlemen, to spare me these few moments; there is no reason why we should not exchange fancies while the law permits. I look upon you as my friends, and I want you to understand the right way of regarding my present position.

Gentlemen of the jury – for *you* deserve to be so called – I have had a remarkable experience. In the past the prophetic voice to which I have become accustomed has always been my constant companion, opposing me even in quite trivial things if I was going to take the wrong course. Now something has happened to me, as you can see, which might be thought and is commonly considered to be a supreme calamity; yet neither when I left home this morning, nor when I was taking my place here in the court, nor at any point in any part of my speech did the divine sign oppose me. In other discussions it has often checked me in the middle of a sentence; but this time it has never opposed me in any part of this business in anything that I have said or done. What do I suppose to be the explanation? I will tell you. I suspect that this thing that has happened to me is a blessing, and we are quite mistaken in supposing death to be an evil. I have good grounds for thinking this, because my accustomed sign could not have failed to oppose me if what I was doing had not been sure to bring some good result.

We should reflect that there is much reason to hope for a good result on other grounds as well. Death is one of two things. Either it is annihilation, and the dead have no consciousness of anything; or, as we are told,[40] it is really a change: a migration of the soul from this place to another. Now if there is no consciousness but only a dreamless sleep, death must be a marvellous gain. I suppose that if anyone were told to pick out the night on which he slept so soundly as not even to dream, and then to compare it with all the other nights and days of his life, and then were told to say, after due consideration, how many better and happier days and nights than this he had spent in the course of his life – well, I think that the Great King [41] himself, to say nothing of any private person, would find these days and nights easy to count in comparison with the rest. If death is like this, then, I call it gain; because the whole of time, if you look at it in this way, can be regarded as no more than one single night. If on the other hand death is a removal from here to some other place, and if what we are told is true, that all the dead are there, what greater blessing could there be than this, gentlemen? If on arrival in the other world, beyond the reach of our so-called justice, one will find there the true judges who are said to preside in those courts, Minos and Rhadamanthys and Aeacus [42] and Triptolemus [43] and all those other half-divinities who were upright in their earthly life, would that be an unrewarding journey? Put it in this way: how much would one of you give to meet Orpheus [44] and Musaeus,[45] Hesiod [46] and Homer? I am willing to die ten times over if this account is true. It would be a specially interesting experience for me to join them there, to meet Palamedes [47] and Ajax [48] the son of Telamon and any other heroes of the old days who met their death through an unfair trial, and to compare my fortunes with theirs – it would be rather amusing, I think–; and above all I should like to spend my time there, as here, in examining and searching people's minds, to find out who is really wise among them, and who only thinks that he is. What would one not give, gentlemen, to be able to question the leader of that great host against Troy, or Odysseus, or Sisyphus,[49] or the thousands of other men and women whom one could mention, to talk and mix and argue with whom would be unimaginable happiness? At any rate I presume that they do not put one to death there for such conduct; because apart from the other happiness in which their world surpasses ours, they are now immortal for the rest of time, if what we are told is true.

You too, gentlemen of the jury, must look forward to death with confidence, and fix your minds on this one belief, which is certain: that nothing can harm a good man either in life or after death, and his fortunes are not a matter of indifference to the gods. This present experience of mine has not come about mechanically; I am quite clear that the time had come when it was better for me to die and be released from my distractions. That is why my sign never turned me back. For my own part I bear no grudge at all against those who condemned me and accused me, although it was not with this kind intention that they did so, but because they thought that they were hurting me; and that is culpable of them. However, I ask them to grant me one favour. When my sons grow up, gentlemen, if you think that they are putting money or anything else before goodness, take your revenge by plaguing them as I plagued you; and if they fancy themselves for no reason, you must scold them just as I scolded you, for neglecting the important things and thinking that they are good for something when they are good for nothing. If you do this, I shall have had justice at your hands, both I myself and my children.

Now it is time that we were going, I to die and you to live; but which of us has the happier prospect is unknown to anyone but God.

SOCRATES IN PRISON

At Athens sentence of execution was normally carried out at once; but the day before Socrates' trial was also the first day of the annual Mission to Delos: a ceremony intended to commemorate the exploit of Theseus when he delivered Athens from the yearly tribute of sending young men and women as food for the Cretan Minotaur. While the State galley was absent on this mission the death penalty could not be inflicted. This year the mission took so long that Socrates was kept in prison for a month.

Some delay in the execution must have been foreseen; and it is possible that Socrates' enemies expected or intended that he should escape and leave the country. His friends certainly urged him to do so. Socrates refused.

The implications of the dialogue have already been outlined in the Introduction, and it may now be left to speak for itself – apart from a few stage directions which have been added to assist the imagination.

CRITO

(SCENE: *A room in the State prison at Athens in the year* 399
B.C. *The time is half an hour before dawn, and the room would be
almost dark but for the light of a little oil lamp. There is a pallet
bed against the back wall. At the head of it a small table supports
the lamp; near the foot of it* CRITO *is sitting patiently on a stool.
He is an old man, kindly, practical, simple-minded; at present he is
suffering from acute emotional strain. On the bed lies* SOCRATES
asleep. He stirs, yawns, opens his eyes and sees CRITO.)

SOCRATES: Here already, Crito? Surely it is still early?
CRITO: Indeed it is.
SOCRATES: About what time?
CRITO: Just before dawn.
SOCRATES: I wonder that the warder paid any attention to
you.
CRITO: He is used to me now, Socrates, because I come
here so often; besides, he is under some small obligation
to me.
SOCRATES: Have you only just come, or have you been
here for long?
CRITO: Fairly long.
SOCRATES: Then why didn't you wake me at once, instead
of sitting by my bed so quietly?
CRITO: I wouldn't dream of such a thing, Socrates. I only
wish I were not so sleepless and depressed myself. I have
been wondering at you, because I saw how comfortably
you were sleeping; and I deliberately didn't wake you because I wanted you to go on being as comfortable as you
could. I have often felt before in the course of my life
how fortunate you are in your disposition, but I feel it
more than ever now in your present misfortune when I
see how easily and placidly you put up with it.

SOCRATES: Well, really, Crito, it would be hardly suitable for a man of my age to resent having to die.

CRITO: Other people just as old as you are get involved in these misfortunes, Socrates, but their age doesn't keep them from resenting it when they find themselves in your position.

SOCRATES: Quite true. But tell me, why have you come so early?

CRITO: Because I bring bad news, Socrates; not so bad from your point of view, I suppose, but it will be very hard to bear for me and your other friends, and I think that I shall find it hardest of all.

SOCRATES: Why, what is this news? Has the boat come in from Delos – the boat which ends my reprieve when it arrives?

CRITO: It hasn't actually come in yet, but I expect that it will be here to-day, judging from the report of some people who have just arrived from Sunium [1] and left it there. It's quite clear from their account that it will be here to-day; and so by to-morrow, Socrates, you will have to – to end your life.

SOCRATES: Well, Crito, I hope that it may be for the best; if the gods will it so, so be it. All the same, I don't think it will arrive to-day.

CRITO: What makes you think that?

SOCRATES: I will try to explain. I think I am right in saying that I have to die on the day after the boat arrives?

CRITO: That's what the authorities say, at any rate.

SOCRATES: Then I don't think it will arrive on this day that is just beginning, but on the day after. I am going by a dream that I had in the night, only a little while ago. It looks as though you were right not to wake me up.

CRITO: Why, what was the dream about?

SOCRATES: I thought I saw a gloriously beautiful woman dressed in white robes, who came up to me and addressed me in these words: 'Socrates,

To the pleasant land of Phthia on the third day thou shalt come.' [2]

CRITO: Your dream makes no sense, Socrates.

SOCRATES: To my mind, Crito, it is perfectly clear.

CRITO: Too clear, apparently. But look here, Socrates, it is still not too late to take my advice and escape. Your death means a double calamity for me. I shall not only lose a friend whom I can never possibly replace, but besides a great many people who don't know you and me very well will be sure to think that I let you down, because I could have saved you if I had been willing to spend the money; and what could be more contemptible than to get a name for thinking more of money than of your friends? Most people will never believe that it was you who refused to leave this place although we tried our hardest to persuade you.

SOCRATES: But my dear Crito, why should we pay so much attention to what 'most people' think? The really reasonable people, who have more claim to be considered, will believe that the facts are exactly as they are.

CRITO: You can see for yourself, Socrates, that one has to think of popular opinion as well. Your present position is quite enough to show that the capacity of ordinary people for causing trouble is not confined to petty annoyances, but has hardly any limits if you once get a bad name with them.

SOCRATES: I only wish that ordinary people *had* an unlimited capacity for doing harm; then they might have an unlimited power for doing good; which would be a splendid thing, if it were so. Actually they have neither. They cannot make a man wise or stupid; they simply act at random.

CRITO: Have it that way if you like; but tell me this, Socrates. I hope that you aren't worrying about the possible effects on me and the rest of your friends, and thinking that if you escape we shall have trouble with informers for having helped you to get away, and have to forfeit all our property or pay an enormous fine, or even incur some further punishment? If any idea like that is troubling you, you can dismiss it altogether. We are quite entitled to run that risk in saving you, and even worse, if necessary. Take my advice, and be reasonable.

SOCRATES: All that you say is very much in my mind, Crito, and a great deal more besides.

CRITO: Very well, then, don't let it distress you. I know some people who are willing to rescue you from here and get you out of the country for quite a moderate sum. And then surely you realize how cheap these informers are to buy off; we shan't need much money to settle them; and I think you've got enough of my money for yourself already. And then even supposing that in your anxiety for my safety you feel that you oughtn't to spend my money, there are these foreign gentlemen staying in Athens who are quite willing to spend theirs. One of them, Simmias of Thebes, has actually brought the money with him for this very purpose; and Cebes [3] and a number of others are quite ready to do the same. So as I say, you mustn't let any fears on these grounds make you slacken your efforts to escape; and you mustn't feel any misgivings about what you said at your trial, that you wouldn't know what to do with yourself if you left this country. Wherever you go, there are plenty of places where you will find a welcome; and if you choose to go to Thessaly, I have friends there who will make much of you and give you complete protection, so that no one in Thessaly can interfere with you.

Besides, Socrates, I don't even feel that it is right for you to try to do what you are doing, throwing away your life when you might save it. You are doing your best to treat yourself in exactly the same way as your enemies would, or rather did, when they wanted to ruin you. What is more, it seems to me that you are letting your sons down too. You have it in your power to finish their bringing up and education, and instead of that you are proposing to go off and desert them, and so far as you are concerned they will have to take their chance. And what sort of chance are they likely to get? The sort of thing that usually happens to orphans when they lose their parents. Either one ought not to have children at all, or one ought to see their upbringing and education through to the end. It strikes me that you are taking the line of least resistance, whereas you ought to make the choice of a good man and a brave one, considering that you profess to have made goodness your object all through life. Really, I am ashamed, both on your account and on ours your friends'; it will look as though we had played something like a coward's part all through this affair of yours. First there was the way you came into court when it was quite unnecessary [4] – that was the first act; then there was the conduct of the defence – that was the second; and finally, to complete the farce, we get this situation, which makes it appear that we have let you slip out of our hands through some lack of courage and enterprise on our part, because we didn't save you, and you didn't save yourself, when it would have been quite possible and practicable, if we had been any use at all.

There, Socrates; if you aren't careful, besides the suffering there will be all this disgrace for you and us to bear. Come, make up your mind. Really it's too late for that now; you ought to have it made up already. There is no alternative; the whole thing must be carried through during this coming night. If we lose any more time, it can't be done, it will be too late. I appeal to you, Socrates, on every ground; take my advice and please don't be unreasonable!

SOCRATES: My dear Crito, I appreciate your warm feelings very much – that is, assuming that they have some justification; if not, the stronger they are, the harder they will be to deal with. Very well, then; we must consider whether we ought to follow your advice or not. You know that this is not a new idea of mine; it has always been my nature never to accept advice from any of my friends unless reflexion shows that it is the best course that reason offers. I cannot abandon the principles which I used to hold in the past simply because this accident has happened to me; they seem to me to be much as they were, and I respect and regard the same principles now as before. So unless we can find better principles on this occasion, you can be quite sure that I shall not agree with you; not even if the power of the people conjures up fresh hordes of bogies to terrify our childish minds, by subjecting us to chains and executions and confiscations of our property.

Well, then, how can we consider the question most reasonably? Suppose that we begin by reverting to this view which you hold about people's opinions. Was it always right to argue that some opinions should be taken seriously but not others? Or was it always wrong? Perhaps it was right before the question of my death arose, but now we can see clearly that it was a mistaken persistence in a point of view which was really irresponsible nonsense. I should like very much to inquire into this problem, Crito, with your help, and to see whether the argument will appear in any different light to me now that I am in this position, or whether it will remain the same; and whether we shall dismiss it or accept it.

Serious thinkers, I believe, have always held some such view as the one which I mentioned just now: that some of the opinions which people entertain should be respected, and others should not. Now I ask you, Crito, don't you think that this is a sound principle? – You are safe from the prospect of dying to-morrow, in all human probability; and you are not likely to have your judgement upset by this impending calamity. Consider, then; don't you think that this is a sound enough principle, that one should not regard all the opinions that people hold, but only some and not others? What do you say? Isn't that a fair statement?

CRITO: Yes, it is.

SOCRATES: In other words, one should regard the good ones and not the bad?

CRITO: Yes.

SOCRATES: The opinions of the wise being good, and the opinions of the foolish bad?

CRITO: Naturally.

SOCRATES: To pass on, then: what do you think of the sort of illustration that I used to employ? When a man is in training, and taking it seriously, does he pay attention to all praise and criticism and opinion indiscriminately, or only when it comes from the one qualified person, the actual doctor or trainer?

CRITO: Only when it comes from the one qualified person.

SOCRATES: Then he should be afraid of the criticism and welcome the praise of the one qualified person, but not those of the general public.

CRITO: Obviously.

SOCRATES: So he ought to regulate his actions and exercises and eating and drinking by the judgement of his instructor, who has expert knowledge, rather than by the opinions of the rest of the public.

CRITO: Yes, that is so.

SOCRATES: Very well. Now if he disobeys the one man and disregards his opinion and commendations, and pays attention to the advice of the many who have no expert knowledge, surely he will suffer some bad effect?

CRITO: Certainly.

SOCRATES: And what is this bad effect? Where is it produced? – I mean, in what part of the disobedient person?

CRITO: His body, obviously; that is what suffers.

SOCRATES: Very good. Well now, tell me, Crito – we don't want to go through all the examples one by one – does this apply as a general rule, and above all to the sort of actions which we are trying to decide about: just and unjust, honourable and dishonourable, good and bad?

Ought we to be guided and intimidated by the opinion of the many or by that of the one – assuming that there is someone with expert knowledge? Is it true that we ought to respect and fear this person more than all the rest put together; and that if we do not follow his guidance we shall spoil and mutilate that part of us which, as we used to say, is improved by right conduct and destroyed by wrong? Or is this all nonsense?

CRITO: No, I think it is true, Socrates.

SOCRATES: Then consider the next step. There is a part of us which is improved by healthy actions and ruined by unhealthy ones. If we spoil it by taking the advice of non-experts, will life be worth living when this part is once ruined? The part I mean is the body; do you accept this?

CRITO: Yes.

SOCRATES: Well, is life worth living with a body which is worn out and ruined in health?

CRITO: Certainly not.

SOCRATES: What about the part of us which is mutilated by wrong actions and benefited by right ones? Is life worth living with this part ruined? Or do we believe that this part of us, whatever it may be, in which right and wrong operate, is of less importance than the body?

CRITO: Certainly not.

SOCRATES: It is really more precious?

CRITO: Much more.

SOCRATES: In that case, my dear fellow, what we ought to consider is not so much what people in general will say about us but how we stand with the expert in right and wrong, the one authority, who represents the actual truth. So in the first place your proposition is not correct when you say that we should consider popular opinion in questions of what is right and honourable and good, or the opposite. Of course one might object 'All the same, the people have the power to put us to death.'

CRITO: No doubt about that! Quite true, Socrates; it is a possible objection.

SOCRATES: But so far as I can see, my dear fellow, the argument which we have just been through is quite unaffected by it. At the same time I should like you to consider whether we are still satisfied on this point: that the really important thing is not to live, but to live well.

CRITO: Why, yes.

SOCRATES: And that to live well means the same thing as to live honourably or rightly?

CRITO: Yes.

SOCRATES: Then in the light of this agreement we must consider whether or not it is right for me to try to get away without an official discharge. If it turns out to be right, we must make the attempt; if not, we must let it drop. As for the considerations you raise about expense and reputation and bringing up children, I am afraid, Crito, that they represent the reflexions of the ordinary public, who put people to death, and would bring them back to life if they could, with equal indifference to reason. Our real duty, I fancy, since the argument leads that way, is to consider one question only, the one which we raised just now: Shall we be acting rightly in paying money and showing gratitude to these people who are going to rescue me, and in escaping or arranging the escape ourselves, or shall we really be acting wrongly in doing all this? If it becomes clear that such conduct is wrong, I cannot help thinking that the question whether we are sure to die, or to suffer any other ill effect for that matter, if we stand our ground and take no action, ought not to weigh with us at all in comparison with the risk of doing what is wrong.

CRITO: I agree with what you say, Socrates; but I wish you would consider what we ought to *do*.

SOCRATES: Let us look at it together, my dear fellow; and if you can challenge any of my arguments, do so and I will listen to you; but if you can't, be a good fellow and stop telling me over and over again that I ought to leave this place without official permission. I am very anxious to obtain your approval before I adopt the course which I have in mind; I don't want to act against your convictions. Now give your attention to the starting point of this inquiry – I hope that you will be satisfied with my way of stating it – and try to answer my questions to the best of your judgement.

CRITO: Well, I will try.

SOCRATES: Do we say that one must never willingly do wrong, or does it depend upon circumstances? Is it true, as we have often agreed before, that there is no sense in which wrongdoing is good or honourable? Or have we jettisoned all our former convictions in these last few days? Can you and I at our age, Crito, have spent all these years in serious discussions without realizing that we were no better than a pair of children? Surely the truth is just what we have always said. Whatever the popular view is, and whether the alternative is pleasanter than the present one or even harder to bear, the fact remains that to do wrong is in every sense bad and dishonourable for the person who does it. Is that our view, or not?

CRITO: Yes, it is.

SOCRATES: Then in no circumstances must one do wrong.

CRITO: No.

SOCRATES: In that case one must not even do wrong when one is wronged, which most people regard as the natural course.

CRITO: Apparently not.

SOCRATES: Tell me another thing, Crito: ought one to do injuries or not?

CRITO: Surely not, Socrates.

SOCRATES: And tell me: is it right to do an injury in retaliation, as most people believe, or not?

CRITO: No, never.

SOCRATES: Because, I suppose, there is no difference between injuring people and wronging them.

CRITO: Exactly.

SOCRATES: So one ought not to return a wrong or an injury to any person, whatever the provocation is. Now be careful, Crito, that in making these single admissions you do not end by admitting something contrary to your real beliefs. I know that there are and always will be few people who think like this; and consequently between those who do think so and those who do not there can be no agreement on principle; they must always feel contempt when they observe one another's decisions. I want even you to consider very carefully whether you share my views and agree with me, and whether we can proceed with our discussion from the established hypothesis that it is never right to do a wrong or return a wrong or defend one's self against injury by retaliation; or whether you dissociate yourself from any share in this view as a basis for discussion. I have held it for a long time, and still hold it; but if you have formed any other opinion, say so and tell me what it is. If, on the other hand, you stand by what we have said, listen to my next point.

CRITO: Yes, I stand by it and agree with you. Go on.

SOCRATES: Well, here is my next point, or rather question. Ought one to fulfil all one's agreements, provided that they are right, or break them?

CRITO: One ought to fulfil them.

SOCRATES: Then consider the logical consequence. If we leave this place without first persuading the State to let us go, are we or are we not doing an injury, and doing it in a quarter where it is least justifiable? Are we or are we not abiding by our just agreements?

CRITO: I can't answer your question, Socrates; I am not clear in my mind.

SOCRATES: Look at it in this way. Suppose that while we were preparing to run away from here (or however one should describe it) the Laws and Constitution of Athens were to come and confront us and ask this question: 'Now, Socrates, what are you proposing to do? Can you deny that by this act which you are contemplating you intend, so far as you have the power, to destroy us, the

Laws, and the whole State as well? Do you imagine that a city can continue to exist and not be turned upside down, if the legal judgements which are pronounced in it have no force but are nullified and destroyed by private persons?' – how shall we answer this question, Crito, and others of the same kind? There is much that could be said, especially by a professional advocate, to protest against the invalidation of this law which enacts that judgements once pronounced shall be binding. Shall we say 'Yes, I do intend to destroy the laws, because the State wronged me by passing a faulty judgement at my trial'? Is this to be our answer, or what?

CRITO: What you have just said, by all means, Socrates.

SOCRATES: Then what supposing the Laws say 'Was there provision for this in the agreement between you and us, Socrates? Or did you undertake to abide by whatever judgements the State pronounced?' If we expressed surprise at such language, they would probably say: 'Never mind our language, Socrates, but answer our questions; after all, you are accustomed to the method of question and answer. Come now, what charge do you bring against us and the State, that you are trying to destroy us? Did we not give you life in the first place? was it not through us that your father married your mother and begot you? Tell us, have you any complaint against those of us Laws that deal with marriage?' 'No, none', I should say. 'Well, have you any against the laws which deal with children's upbringing and education, such as you had yourself? Are you not grateful to those of us Laws which were instituted for this end, for requiring your father to give you a cultural and physical education?' 'Yes', I should say. 'Very good. Then since you have been born and brought up and educated, can you deny, in the first place, that you were our child and servant, both you and your ancestors? And if this is so, do you imagine that what is right for us is equally right for you, and that whatever we try to do to you, you are justified in retaliating? You did not have equality of rights with your father, or your employer (supposing that you had had one), to enable you to retaliate; you were not allowed to answer back when you were scolded or to hit back when you were beaten, or to do a great many other things of the same kind. Do you expect to have such licence against your country and its laws that if we try to put you to death in the belief that it is right to do so, you on your part will try your hardest to destroy your country and us its Laws in return? and will you, the true devotee of goodness, claim that you are justified in doing so? Are you so wise as to have forgotten that compared with your mother and father and all the rest of your ancestors your country is something far more precious, more venerable, more sacred, and held in greater honour both among gods and among all reasonable men? Do you not realize that you are even more bound to respect and placate the anger of your country than your father's anger? that if you cannot persuade your country you must do whatever it orders, and patiently submit to any punishment that it imposes, whether it be flogging or imprisonment? And if it leads you out to war, to be wounded or killed, you must comply, and it is right that you should do so; you must not give way or retreat or abandon your position. Both in war and in the law-courts and everywhere else you must do whatever your city and your country commands, or else persuade it in accordance with universal justice; but violence is a sin even against your parents, and it is a far greater sin against your country.' – What shall we say to this, Crito? – that what the Laws say is true, or not?

RITO: Yes, I think so.

SOCRATES: 'Consider, then, Socrates,' the Laws would probably continue, 'whether it is also true for us to say that what you are now trying to do to us is not right. Although we have brought you into the world and reared you and educated you, and given you and all your fellow-citizens a share in all the good things at our disposal, nevertheless by the very fact of granting our permission we openly proclaim this principle: that any Athenian, on attaining to manhood and seeing for himself the political organization of the state and us its Laws, is permitted, if he is not satisfied with us, to take his property and go away wherever he likes. If any of you chooses to go to one of our colonies, supposing that he should not be satisfied with us and the State, or to emigrate to any other country, not one of us Laws hinders or prevents him from going away wherever he likes, without any loss of property. On the other hand, if any one of you stands his ground when he can see how we administer justice and the rest of our public organization, we hold that by so doing he has in fact undertaken to do anything that we tell him; and we maintain that anyone who disobeys is guilty of doing wrong on three separate counts: first because we are his parents, and secondly because we are his guardians; and thirdly because, after promising obedience, he is neither obeying us nor persuading us to change our decision if we are at fault in any way; and although all our orders are in the form of proposals, not of savage commands, and we give him the choice of either persuading us or doing what we say, he is actually doing neither. These are the charges, Socrates, to which we say that you will be liable if you do what you are contemplating; and you will not be the least culpable of your fellow-countrymen, but one of the most guilty.' If I said 'Why do you say that?' they would no doubt pounce upon me with perfect justice and point out that there are very few people in Athens who have entered into this agreement with them as explicitly as I have. They would say 'Socrates, we have substantial evidence that you are satisfied with us and with the State. You would not have been so exceptionally reluctant to cross the borders of your country if you had not been exceptionally attached to it. You have never left the city to attend a festival or for any other purpose, except on some military expedition; you have never travelled abroad as other people do, and you have never felt the impulse to acquaint yourself with another country or constitution; you have been content with us and with our city. You have definitely chosen us, and undertaken to observe us in all your activities as a citizen; and as the crowning proof that you are satisfied with our city, you have begotten children in it. Furthermore, even at the time of your trial you could have proposed the penalty of banishment, if you had chosen to do so; that is, you could have done then with the sanction of the State what you are now trying to do without it. But whereas at that time you made a noble show of indifference if you had to die, and in fact preferred death, as you said, to banishment, now you show no respect for your earlier professions, and no regard for us, the Laws, whom you are trying to destroy; you are behaving like the lowest type of menial, trying to run away in spite of the contracts and undertakings by which you agreed to live as a member of our State. Now first answer this question: Are we or are we not speaking the truth when we say that you have undertaken, in deed if not in word, to live your life as a citizen in obedience to us?' What are we to say to that, Crito? Are we not bound to admit it?

CRITO: We cannot help it, Socrates.

SOCRATES:'It is a fact, then,' they would say, 'that you are breaking covenants and undertakings made with us, although you made them under no compulsion or misunderstanding, and were not compelled to decide in a limited time; you had seventy years in which you could have left the country, if you were not satisfied with us or felt that the agreements were unfair. You did not choose Sparta or Crete [5] – your favourite models of good government – or any other Greek or foreign state; you could not have absented yourself from the city less if you had been lame or blind or decrepit in some other way.

It is quite obvious that you stand by yourself above all other Athenians in your affection for this city and for us its Laws; – who would care for a city without laws? And now, after all this, are you not going to stand by your agreement? Yes, you are, Socrates, if you will take our advice; and then you will at least escape being laughed at for leaving the city.

'We invite you to consider what good you will do to yourself or your friends if you commit this breach of faith and stain your conscience. It is fairly obvious that the risk of being banished and either losing their citizenship or having their property confiscated will extend to your friends as well. As for yourself, if you go to one of the neighbouring states, such as Thebes or Megara,[6] which are both well governed, you will enter them as an enemy to their constitution,[7] and all good patriots will eye you with suspicion as a destroyer of law and order. Incidentally you will confirm the opinion of the jurors who tried you that they gave a correct verdict; a destroyer of laws might very well be supposed to have a destructive influence upon young and foolish human beings. Do you intend, then, to avoid well governed states and the higher forms of human society? and if you do, will life be worth living? Or will you approach these people and have the impudence to converse with them? What arguments will you use, Socrates? The same which you used here, that goodness and integrity, institutions and laws, are the most precious possessions of mankind? Do you not think that Socrates and everything about him will appear in a disreputable light? You certainly ought to think so. But perhaps you will retire from this part of the world and go to Crito's friends in Thessaly? That is the home of indiscipline and laxity, and no doubt they would enjoy hearing the amusing story of how you managed to run away from prison by arraying yourself in some costume or putting on a shepherd's smock or some other conventional runaway's disguise, and altering

your personal appearance. And will no one comment on
the fact that an old man of your age, probably with only a
short time left to live, should dare to cling so greedily to
life, at the price of violating the most stringent laws?
Perhaps not, if you avoid irritating anyone. Otherwise,
Socrates, you will hear a good many humiliating comments. So you will live as the toady and slave of all the
populace, literally "roystering in Thessaly",[8] as though
you had left this country for Thessaly to attend a banquet
there; and where will your discussions about goodness
and uprightness be then, we should like to know? But
of course you want to live for your children's sake, so
that you may be able to bring them up and educate them.
Indeed! by first taking them off to Thessaly and making
foreigners of them, so that they may have that additional
enjoyment? Or if that is not your intention, supposing
that they are brought up here with you still alive, will
they be better cared for and educated without you, because of course your friends will look after them? Will
they look after your children if you go away to Thessaly,
and not if you go away to the next world? Surely if those
who profess to be your friends are worth anything, you
must believe that they would care for them.

'No, Socrates; be advised by us your guardians, and
do not think more of your children or of your life or of
anything else than you think of what is right; so that
when you enter the next world you may have all this to
plead in your defence before the authorities there. It
seems clear that if you do this thing, neither you nor any
of your friends will be the better for it or be more upright or have a cleaner conscience here in this world, nor
will it be better for you when you reach the next. As it is,
you will leave this place, when you do, as the victim of a
wrong done not by us, the Laws, but by your fellow-
men. But if you leave in that dishonourable way, return-
ing wrong for wrong and evil for evil, breaking your
agreements and covenants with us, and injuring those

whom you least ought to injure – yourself, your friends, your country, and us – then you will have to face our anger in your lifetime, and in that place beyond when the laws of the other world know that you have tried, so far as you could, to destroy even us their brothers, they will not receive you with a kindly welcome. Do not take Crito's advice, but follow ours.'

That, my dear friend Crito, I do assure you, is what I seem to hear them saying, just as a mystic [9] seems to hear the strains of music; and the sound of their arguments rings so loudly in my head that I cannot hear the other side. I warn you that, as my opinion stands at present, it will be useless to urge a different view. However, if you think that you will do any good by it, say what you like.

CRITO: No, Socrates, I have nothing to say.

SOCRATES: Then give it up, Crito, and let us follow this course, since God points out the way.

THE LAST CONVERSATION

The story of Socrates' last day in prison is told by an eye-witness,
Phaedo of Elis, to a group of sympathetic fellow-philosophers, only
one of whom – Echecrates – is named and speaks. The scene of their
conversation is laid in Phlius, a little town in the north-east of the
Peloponnese. Thus the Phaedo *is a reported dialogue, or one*
dialogue inside another. (The artistic advantages of this form will
be clearly seen and need not be laboured.) But it is more than a mere
description of what was said and done, and more than a tribute to
a noble death. It is an attempt to encourage by every means a belief
in the soul's immortality – not to prove it by logic, for Plato knew
quite well that this is impossible, but to commend it to intuition.
If in this attempt he went beyond the literal facts, he is no more to
be censured than a portrait-painter who reveals more than the
physical appearance of his subject; for the belief in immortality is
to be our inspiration to obey the master's solemn command: to live
the life of the true philosopher. The Phaedo *is indeed the testament*
of Socrates.

ANALYSIS OF THE PHAEDO

PHAEDO

ECHECRATES: Were you there with Socrates yourself, Phaedo, when he was executed, or did you hear about it from somebody else?

PHAEDO: No, I was there myself, Echecrates.

ECHECRATES: Then what did the Master say before he died, and how did he meet his end? I should very much like to know. None of the people in Phlius go to Athens much in these days, and it is a long time since we had any visitor from there who could give us any definite information, except that he was executed by drinking hemlock [1]; nobody could tell us anything more than that.

PHAEDO: Then haven't you even heard how his trial went?

ECHECRATES: Yes, someone told us about that; and we were surprised because there was obviously a long interval between it and the execution. How was that, Phaedo?

PHAEDO: A fortunate coincidence, Echecrates. It so happened that on the day before the trial they had just finished garlanding the stern of the ship which Athens sends to Delos.

ECHECRATES: What ship is that?

PHAEDO: The Athenians say that it is the one in which Theseus sailed away to Crete with the seven youths and seven maidens, and saved their lives and his own as well. The story says that the Athenians made a vow to Apollo that if these young people's lives were saved they would send a solemn mission to Delos every year; and ever since then they have kept their vow to the God, right down to the present day. They have a law that as soon as this mission begins the city must be kept pure, and no public executions may take place until the ship has reached Delos and returned again; which sometimes takes a long time, if the winds happen to hold it back. The mission is considered to begin as soon as the priest of Apollo has

99

garlanded the stern of the ship; and this happened, as I say, on the day before the trial. That is why Socrates spent such a long time in prison between his trial and execution.

ECHECRATES: But what about the actual circumstances of his death, Phaedo? What was said and done, and which of the Master's companions were with him? Or did the authorities refuse them admission, so that he passed away without a friend at his side?

PHAEDO: Oh no; some of them were there – quite a number, in fact.

ECHECRATES: I wish you would be kind enough to give us a really detailed account – unless you are pressed for time.

PHAEDO: No, not at all. I will try to describe it for you. Nothing gives me more pleasure than recalling the memory of Socrates, either by talking myself or by listening to someone else.

ECHECRATES: Well, Phaedo, you will find that your audience feels just the same about it. Now try to describe every detail as carefully as you can.

PHAEDO: In the first place, my own feelings at the time were quite extraordinary. It never occurred to me to feel sorry for him, as you might have expected me to feel at the deathbed of a very dear friend. The Master seemed quite happy, Echecrates, both in his manner and in what he said; he met his death so fearlessly and nobly. I could not help feeling that even on his way to the other world he would be under the providence of God, and that when he arrived there all would be well with him, if it ever has been so with anybody. So I felt no sorrow at all, as you might have expected on such a solemn occasion; and at the same time I felt no pleasure at being occupied in our usual philosophical discussions – that was the form that our conversation took –; I felt an absolutely incomprehensible emotion, a sort of curious blend of pleasure and pain combined, as my mind took it in that in a little while my friend was going to die. All of us who were there were affected in much the same way, between laughing and crying; one of us in particular, Apollodorus – you know what he is like, don't you?

ECHECRATES: Of course I do.

PHAEDO: Well, he quite lost control of himself; and I and the others were very much upset.

ECHECRATES: Who were actually there, Phaedo?

PHAEDO: Why, of the local people there were this man Apollodorus,[2] and Critobulus [3] and his father, and then there were Hermogenes and Epigenes and Aeschines and Antisthenes. Oh yes, and Ctesippus of Paeanis, and Menexenus, and some other local people. I believe that Plato was ill.

ECHECRATES: Were there any visitors from outside?

PHAEDO: Yes: Simmias of Thebes, with Cebes [4] and Phaedondas; and Euclides and Terpsion from Megara.

ECHECRATES: Why, weren't Aristippus and Cleombrotus there?

PHAEDO: No, they were in Aegina, apparently.

ECHECRATES: Was there anybody else?

PHAEDO: I think that's about all.

ECHECRATES: Well, what form did the discussion take?

PHAEDO: I will try to tell you all about it from the very beginning. We had all made it our regular practice, even in the period before, to visit Socrates every day; we used to meet at daybreak by the court-house where the trial was held, because it was close to the prison. We always spent some time in conversation while we waited for the door to open, which was never very early; and when it did open, we used to go in to see Socrates, and generally spent the day with him. On this particular day we met earlier than usual, because when we left the prison on the evening before, we heard that the boat had just arrived back from Delos; so we urged one another to meet at the same place as early as possible. When we arrived, the porter, instead of letting us in as usual, told us to wait and not to come in until he gave us the word. 'The commissioners are taking off Socrates' chains,' he said, 'and warning him that he is to die to-day.' After a short interval he came back and told us to go in.

When we went inside we found Socrates just released from his chains, and Xanthippe [5] – you know her! – sitting by him with the little boy on her knee. As soon as Xanthippe saw us she broke out into the sort of remark you would expect from a woman: 'Oh, Socrates, this is the last time that you and your friends will be able to talk together!' Socrates looked at Crito. 'Crito,' he said, 'someone had better take her home.' Some of Crito's servants led her away crying hysterically.

Socrates sat up on the bed and drew up his leg and massaged it, saying as he did so 'What a queer thing it is, my friends, this sensation which is popularly called pleasure! It is remarkable how closely it is connected with its conventional opposite, pain. They will never come to a man both at once, but if you pursue one of them and catch it, you are nearly always compelled to have the other as well; they are like two bodies attached to the same head. I am sure that if Aesop had thought of it he would have made up a fable about them, something like this: God wanted to stop their continual quarrelling, and when he found that it was impossible, he fastened their heads together; so wherever one of them appears, the other is sure to follow after. That is exactly what seems to be happening to me. I had a pain in my leg from the fetter, and now I feel the pleasure coming that follows it.'

Here Cebes broke in and said 'Oh yes, Socrates, I am glad you reminded me. Evenus asked me a day or two ago, as others have done before, about the lyrics which you have been composing lately by adapting Aesop's fables and the Prelude to Apollo; he wanted to know what induced you to write them now after you had gone to prison, when you had never done anything of the kind before. If you would like me to be able to answer Evenus when he asks me again – as I am sure he will – tell me what I am to say.'

'Tell him the truth,' said Socrates, 'that I did not compose them to rival either him or his poetry – which I knew would not be easy; I did it in the attempt to discover the meaning of certain dreams, and to clear my conscience, in case this was the art which I had been told to practise. It is like this, you see. In the course of my life I have often had the same dream, appearing in different forms at different times, but always saying the same thing: "Socrates, practise and cultivate the arts". In the past I used to think that it was impelling and exhorting me to do what I was actually doing; I mean that the dream, like a spectator encouraging a runner in a race, was urging me on to do what I was doing already, that is, practising the arts; because philosophy is the greatest of the arts, and I was practising it. But ever since my trial, while the festival of the god has been delaying my execution, I have felt that perhaps it might be this popular form of art that the dream intended me to practise, in which case I ought to practise it and not disobey; I thought it would be safer not to take my departure before I had cleared my conscience by writing poetry and so obeying the dream. I began with some verses in honour of the god whose festival it was. When I had finished my hymn, I reflected that a poet, if he is to be worthy of the name, ought to work on imaginative themes, not descriptive ones; and I was not good at inventing stories. So I availed myself of some of Aesop's fables which were ready to hand and familiar to me, and I versified the first of them that suggested themselves. You can tell Evenus this, Cebes, and bid him farewell from me, and tell him, if he is wise, to follow me as quickly as he can. I shall be going to-day, it seems; those are my country's orders.'

'What a piece of advice for Evenus, Socrates!' said

Simmias. 'I have had a good deal to do with him before now, and from what I know of him he will not be at all ready to obey you.'

'Why?' he asked. 'Isn't Evenus a philosopher?'

'So I believe,' said Simmias.

'Well then, he will be quite willing, just like anyone else who is properly grounded in philosophy. However, he will hardly do himself violence, because they say that it is not legitimate.' As he spoke he lowered his feet to the ground, and sat like this for the rest of the discussion.

Cebes now asked him 'Socrates, what do you mean by saying that it is not legitimate to do one's self violence, although a philosopher will be willing to follow a friend who dies?'

'Why, Cebes, have you and Simmias never heard about these things while you have been with Philolaus?'

'Nothing definite, Socrates.'

'Well, even my information is only based on hearsay; but I don't mind at all telling you what I have heard. I suppose that for one who is soon to leave this world there is no more suitable occupation than inquiring into our views about the future life, and trying to imagine what it is like. What else can one do in the time before sunset?'

'Tell me then, Socrates, what are the grounds for saying that suicide is not legitimate? I have heard it described as wrong before now (as you suggested) both by Philolaus, when he was staying with us, and by others as well; but I have never yet heard any definite explanation for it.'

'Well, you must not lose heart,' he said; 'perhaps you will hear one some day. However, no doubt you will feel it strange that this should be the one question that has an unqualified answer – I mean, if it never happens in the case of life and death (as it does in all other connexions) that sometimes and for some people death is better than life; and it probably seems strange to you that it should not be right for those to whom death would be an advantage to benefit themselves, but that they should have to await the services of someone else.'

Cebes laughed gently and said 'Aye, that it does,' dropping into his own dialect.

'Yes,' went on Socrates, 'put in that way it certainly might seem unreasonable, though perhaps it has some justification. The allegory [6] which the mystics tell us – that we men are put in a sort of guard-post, from which one must not release one's self or run away – seems to me to be a high doctrine with difficult implications. All the same, Cebes, I believe that this much is true: that the gods are our keepers, and we men are one of their possessions. Don't you think so?'

'Yes, I do,' said Cebes.

'Then take your own case; if one of your possessions were to destroy itself without intimation from you that you wanted it to die, wouldn't you be angry with it and punish it, if you had any means of doing so?'

'Certainly.'

'So if you look at it in this way I suppose it is not unreasonable to say that we must not put an end to ourselves until God sends some compulsion like the one which we are facing now.'

'That seems likely, I admit,' said Cebes. 'But what you were saying just now, that philosophers would be readily willing to die – that seems illogical, Socrates, assuming that we were right in saying a moment ago that God is our keeper and we are his possessions. If this service is directed by the gods, who are the very best of masters, it is inexplicable that the very wisest of men should not be grieved at quitting it; because he surely cannot expect to provide for himself any better when he is free. On the other hand a stupid person might get the idea that it would be to his advantage to escape from his master; he might not reason it out that one should not escape from a good master, but remain with him as long as possible;

and so he might run away unreflectingly. A sensible man would wish to remain always with his superior. If you look at it in this way, Socrates, the probable thing is just the opposite of what we said just now: it is natural for the wise to be grieved when they die, and for fools to be happy.'

When Socrates had listened to this he seemed to me to be amused at Cebes' persistence, and looking round at us he said 'You know, Cebes is always investigating arguments, and he is not at all willing to accept every statement at its face value.'

Simmias said 'Well, but, Socrates, I think that this time there is something in what he says. Why should a really wise man want to desert masters who are better than himself, and to get rid of them so lightly? I think Cebes is aiming his criticism at you, because you are making so light of leaving us, and the gods too, who as you admit are good masters.'

'What you and Cebes say is perfectly fair,' said Socrates. 'You mean, I suppose, that I must make a formal defence against this charge.'

'Exactly,' said Simmias.

'Very well then; let me try to make a more convincing defence to you than I made at my trial. If I did not expect to enter the company, first, of other wise and good gods, and secondly of men now dead who are better than those who are in this world now, it is true that I should be wrong in not grieving at death. As it is, you can be assured that I expect to find myself among good men; I would not insist particularly on this point, but on the other I assure you that I shall insist most strongly: that I shall find there divine masters who are supremely good. That is why I am not so much distressed as I might be, and why I have a firm hope that there is something in store for those who have died, and (as we have been told [7] for many years) something much better for the good than for the wicked.'

'Well, what is your idea, Socrates?' asked Simmias. 'Do you mean to keep this knowledge to yourself now that you are leaving us, or will you communicate it to us too? I think that we ought to have a share in this comfort; besides, it will serve as your defence, if we are satisfied with what you say.'

'Very well, I will try,' he replied. 'But before I begin, Crito here seems to have been wanting to say something for some time; let us find out what it is.'

'Only this, Socrates,' said Crito, 'that the man who is to give you the poison has been asking me for a long time to tell you to talk as little as possible; he says that talking makes you heated, and that you ought not to do anything to affect the action of the poison. Otherwise it is sometimes necessary to take a second dose, or even a third.'

'That is his affair,' said Socrates. 'Let him make his own preparations for administering it twice or three times if necessary.'

'I was pretty sure you would say that,' said Crito, 'but he's been bothering me for a long time.'

'Never mind him,' said Socrates. 'Now for you, my jury. I want to explain to you how it seems to me natural that a man who has really devoted his life to philosophy should be cheerful in the face of death, and confident of finding the greatest blessing in the next world when his life is finished. I will try to make clear to you, Simmias and Cebes, how this can be so.

'Ordinary people seem not to realize that those who really apply themselves in the right way to philosophy are directly and of their own accord preparing themselves for dying and death. If this is true, and they have actually been looking forward to death all their lives, it would of course be absurd to be troubled when the thing comes for which they have so long been preparing and looking forward.'

Simmias laughed and said 'Upon my word, Socrates,

you have made me laugh, though I was not at all in the mood for it. I am sure that if they heard what you said, most people would think – and our fellow-countrymen [8] would heartily agree – that it was a very good hit at the philosophers to say that they are half dead already, and that they, the normal people, are quite aware that death would serve the philosophers right.'

'And they would be quite correct, Simmias; except in thinking that they are "quite aware". They are not at all aware in what sense true philosophers are half dead, or in what sense they deserve death, or what sort of death they deserve. But let us dismiss them and talk among ourselves. Do we believe that there is such a thing as death?'

'Most certainly,' said Simmias, taking up the rôle of answering.

'Is it simply the release of the soul from the body? Is death nothing more or less than this, the separate condition of the body by itself when it is released from the soul, and the separate condition by itself of the soul when released from the body? Is death anything else than this?'

'No, just that.'

'Well then, my boy, see whether you agree with me; I fancy that this will help us to find out the answer to our problem. Do you think that it is right for a philosopher to concern himself with the so-called pleasures connected with food and drink?'

'Certainly not, Socrates,' said Simmias.

'What about sexual pleasures?'

'No, not at all.'

'And what about the other attentions that we pay to our bodies? do you think that a philosopher attaches any importance to them? I mean things like providing himself with smart clothes and shoes and other bodily ornaments; do you think that he values them or despises them – in so far as there is no real necessity for him to go in for that sort of thing?'

'I think the true philosopher despises them,' he said.

'Then it is your opinion in general that a man of this kind is not concerned with the body, but keeps his attention directed as much as he can away from it and towards the soul?'

'Yes, it is.'

'So it is clear first of all in the case of physical pleasures that the philosopher frees his soul from association with the body (so far as is possible) to a greater extent than other men?'

'It seems so.'

'And most people think, do they not, Simmias, that a man who finds no pleasure and takes no part in these things does not deserve to live, and that anyone who thinks nothing of physical pleasures has one foot in the grave?'

'That is perfectly true.'

'Now take the acquisition of knowledge; is the body a hindrance or not, if one takes it into partnership to share an investigation? What I mean is this: is there any certainty in human sight and hearing, or is it true, as the poets are always dinning into our ears, that we neither hear nor see anything accurately? Yet if these senses are not clear and accurate, the rest can hardly be so, because they are all inferior to the first two. Don't you agree?'

'Certainly.'

'Then when is it that the soul attains to truth? When it tries to investigate anything with the help of the body, it is obviously led astray.'

'Quite so.'

'Is it not in the course of reflection, if at all, that the soul gets a clear view of facts?'

'Yes.'

'Surely the soul can best reflect when it is free of all distractions such as hearing or sight or pain or pleasure of any kind – that is, when it ignores the body and becomes

as far as possible independent, avoiding all physical con-
tacts and associations as much as it can, in its search for
reality.'

'That is so.'

'Then here too – in despising the body and avoiding
it, and endeavouring to become independent – the philosopher's soul is ahead of all the rest.'

'It seems so.'

'Here are some more questions, Simmias. Do we
recognize such a thing as absolute uprightness?' [9]

'Indeed we do.'

'And absolute beauty and goodness too?'

'Of course.'

'Have you ever seen any of these things with your
eyes?'

'Certainly not,' said he.

'Well, have you ever apprehended them with any other
bodily sense? By "them" I mean not only absolute tallness or health or strength, but the real nature of any given
thing – what it actually is. Is it through the body that we
get the truest perception of them? Isn't it true that in
any inquiry you are likely to attain more nearly to knowledge of your object in proportion to the care and accur-
acy with which you have prepared yourself to understand that object in itself?'

'Certainly.'

'Don't you think that the person who is likely to succeed in this attempt most perfectly is the one who approaches each object, as far as possible, with the unaided
intellect, without taking account of any sense of sight in
his thinking, or dragging any other sense into his reckon-
ing – the man who pursues the truth by applying his pure
and unadulterated thought to the pure and unadulterated
object, cutting himself off as much as possible from his
eyes and ears and virtually all the rest of his body, as an
impediment which by its presence prevents the soul from
attaining to truth and clear thinking? Is not this the

person, Simmias, who will reach the goal of reality, if anybody can?'

'What you say is absolutely true, Socrates,' said Simmias.

'All these considerations,' said Socrates, 'must surely prompt serious philosophers to review the position in some such way as this. "It looks as though this were a bypath leading to the right track. So long as we keep to the body and our soul is contaminated with this imperfection, there is no chance of our ever attaining satisfactorily to our object, which we assert to be Truth. In the first place, the body provides us with innumerable distractions in the pursuit of our necessary sustenance; and any diseases which attack us hinder our quest for reality. Besides, the body fills us with loves and desires and fears and all sorts of fancies and a great deal of nonsense, with the result that we literally never get an opportunity to think at all about anything. Wars and revolutions and battles are due simply and solely to the body and its desires. All wars are undertaken for the acquisition of wealth; and the reason why we have to acquire wealth is the body, because we are slaves in its service. That is why, on all these accounts, we have so little time for philosophy. Worst of all, if we do obtain any leisure from the body's claims and turn to some line of inquiry, the body intrudes once more into our investigations, interrupting, disturbing, distracting, and preventing us from getting a glimpse of the truth. We are in fact convinced that if we are ever to have pure knowledge of anything, we must get rid of the body and contemplate things by themselves with the soul by itself. It seems, to judge from the argument, that the wisdom which we desire and upon which we profess to have set our hearts will be attainable only when we are dead, and not in our lifetime. If no pure knowledge is possible in the company of the body, then either it is totally impossible to acquire knowledge, or it is only possible after death, because it is only then that the soul will be separate and independent of the body. It seems that so long as we are alive, we shall continue closest to knowledge if we avoid as much as we can all contact and association with the body, except when they are absolutely necessary; and instead of allowing ourselves to become infected with its nature, purify ourselves from it until God himself gives us deliverance. In this way, by keeping ourselves uncontaminated by the follies of the body, we shall probably reach the company of others like ourselves and gain direct knowledge of all that is pure and uncontaminated – that is, presumably, of Truth. For one who is not pure himself to attain to the realm of purity would no doubt be a breach of universal justice." Something to this effect, Simmias, is what I imagine all real lovers of learning must think themselves and say to one another; don't you agree with me?'

'Most emphatically, Socrates.'

'Very well, then,' said Socrates; 'if this is true, there is good reason for anyone who reaches the end of this journey which lies before me to hope that there, if anywhere, he will attain the object to which all our efforts have been directed during my past life. So this journey which is now ordained for me carries a happy prospect for any other man also who believes that his mind has been prepared by purification.'

'It does indeed,' said Simmias.

'And purification, as we saw some time ago in our discussion, consists in separating the soul as much as possible from the body, and accustoming it to withdraw from all contact with the body and concentrate itself by itself; and to have its dwelling, so far as it can, both now and in the future, alone by itself, freed from the shackles of the body. Does not that follow?'

'Yes, it does,' said Simmias.

'Is not what we call death a freeing and separation of soul from body?'

'Certainly,' he said.

'And the desire to free the soul is found chiefly, or rather only, in the true philosopher; in fact the philosopher's occupation consists precisely in the freeing and separation of soul from body. Isn't that so?'

'Apparently.'

'Well then, as I said at the beginning, if a man has trained himself throughout his life to live in a state as close as possible to death, would it not be ridiculous for him to be distressed when death comes to him?'

'It would, of course.'

'Then it is a fact, Simmias, that true philosophers make dying their profession, and that to them of all men death is least alarming. Look at it in this way. If they are thoroughly dissatisfied with the body, and long to have their souls independent of it, when this happens would it not be entirely unreasonable to be frightened and distressed? Would they not naturally be glad to set out for the place where there is a prospect of attaining the object of their lifelong desire, which is Wisdom; and of escaping from an unwelcome association? Surely there are many who have chosen of their own free will to follow dead lovers and wives and sons to the next world, in the hope of seeing and meeting there the persons whom they loved. If this is so, will a true lover of wisdom who has firmly grasped this same conviction – that he will never attain to wisdom worthy of the name elsewhere than in the next world – will he be grieved at dying? Will he not be glad to make that journey? We must suppose so, my dear boy; that is, if he is a real philosopher; because then he will be of the firm belief that he will never find wisdom in all its purity in any other place. If this is so, would it not be quite unreasonable (as I said just now) for such a man to be afraid of death?'

'It would, indeed.'

'So if you see any one distressed at the prospect of dying,' said Socrates, 'it will be proof enough that he is a lover not of wisdom but of the body. As a matter of fact, I suppose he is also a lover of wealth and reputation; one or the other, or both.'

'Yes, you are quite right.'

'Doesn't it follow, Simmias,' he went on, 'that the virtue which we call courage belongs primarily to the philosophical disposition?'

'Yes, no doubt it does,' he said.

'Self-control, too, as it is understood even in the popular sense – not being carried away by the desires, but preserving a decent indifference towards them–: is not this appropriate only to those who regard the body with the greatest indifference and spend their lives in philosophy?'

'Certainly,' he said.

'If you care to consider courage and self-control as practised by other people,' said Socrates, 'you will find them illogical.'

'How so, Socrates?'

'You know, don't you, that everyone except the philosopher regards death as a great evil?'

'Yes, indeed.'

'Isn't it true that when a brave man faces death he does so through fear of something worse?'

'Yes, it is true.'

'So in everyone except the philosopher courage is due to fear and dread; although it is illogical that fear and cowardice should make a man brave.'

'Quite so.'

'What about temperate people? Is it not, in just the same way, a sort of self-indulgence that makes them self-controlled? We may say that this is impossible, but all the same those who practise this simple form of self-control are in much the same case as that which I have just described. They are afraid of losing other pleasures which they desire, so they refrain from one kind because they cannot resist the other. Although they define self-indulgence as the condition of being ruled by pleasure, it is really because they cannot resist some pleasures that they succeed in resisting others; which amounts to what I said just now – that they control themselves, in a sense, by self-indulgence.'

'Yes, that seems to be true.'

'I congratulate you on your perception, Simmias. No, I am afraid that, from the moral standpoint, it is not the right method to exchange one degree of pleasure or pain or fear for another, like coins of different values. There is only one currency for which all these tokens of ours should be exchanged, and that is wisdom. In fact, it is wisdom that makes possible courage and self-control and integrity or, in a word, true goodness, and the presence or absence of pleasures and fears and other such feelings makes no difference at all; whereas a system of morality which is based on relative emotional values is a mere illusion, a thoroughly vulgar conception which has nothing sound in it and nothing true. The true moral ideal, whether self-control or integrity or courage, is really a kind of purgation from all these emotions, and wisdom itself is a sort of purification. Perhaps these people who direct the religious initiations are not so far from the mark, and all the time there has been an allegorical meaning beneath their doctrine that he who enters the next world uninitiated and unenlightened shall lie in the mire, but he who arrives there purified and enlightened shall dwell among the gods. You know how the initiation-practitioners say:

"Many bear the emblems, but the devotees are few"?

Well, in my opinion these devotees are simply those who have lived the philosophic life in the right way; a company which, all through my life, I have done my best in every way to join, leaving nothing undone which I could do to attain this end. Whether I was right in this ambition, and whether we have achieved anything, we shall know for certain (if God wills) when we reach the other world; and that, I imagine, will be fairly soon.

'This is the defence which I offer you, Simmias and Cebes, to show that it is natural for me to leave you and my earthly rulers without any feeling of grief or bitterness, since I believe that I shall find there, no less than here, good rulers and good friends. If I am any more convincing in my defence to you than I was to my Athenian jury, I shall be satisfied.'

When Socrates had finished, Cebes made his reply. 'The rest of your statement, Socrates,' he said, 'seems excellent to me; but what you said about the soul leaves the average person with grave misgivings that when it is released from the body it may no longer exist anywhere, but may be dispersed and destroyed on the very day that the man himself dies, as soon as it is freed from the body; that as it emerges it may be dissipated like breath or smoke, and vanish away, so that nothing is left of it anywhere. Of course if it still existed as an independent unity, released from all the evils which you have just described, there would be a strong and glorious hope, Socrates, that what you say is true. But I fancy that it requires no little faith and assurance to believe that the soul exists after death and retains some active force and intelligence.'

'Quite true, Cebes,' said Socrates. 'But what are we to do about it? Is it your wish that we should go on speculating about the subject, to see whether this view is likely to be true or not?'

'For my part,' said Cebes, 'I should be very glad to hear what you think about it.'

'At any rate,' said Socrates, 'I hardly think that any one who heard us now – even a comic poet [10] – would say that I am wasting time and discoursing on subjects which do not concern me. So if that is how you feel, we had better continue our inquiry. Let us approach it from this point of view: Do the souls of the departed exist in another world or not?

'There is an old legend,[11] which we still remember, to

the effect that they *do* exist there, after leaving here; and that they return again to this world and come into being[12] from the dead. If this is so – that the living come into being again from the dead – does it not follow that our souls exist in the other world? They could not come into being again if they did not exist; and it will be sufficient proof that my contention is true if it really becomes apparent that the living come from the dead, and from nowhere else. But if this is not so, we shall need some other argument.'

'Quite so,' said Cebes.

'If you want to understand the question more readily,' said Socrates, 'consider it with reference not only to human beings but to all animals and plants. Let us see whether in general everything that admits of generation is generated in this way and no other – opposites from opposites, wherever there is an opposite; as for instance beauty is opposite to ugliness and right to wrong, and there are countless other examples. Let us consider whether it is a necessary law that everything which has an opposite is generated from that opposite and from no other source. For example, when a thing becomes bigger, it must, I suppose, have been smaller first before it became bigger?'

'Yes.'

'And similarly if it becomes smaller, it must be bigger first, and become smaller afterwards?'

'That is so,' said Cebes.

'And the weaker comes from the stronger, and the faster from the slower?'

'Certainly.'

'One more instance: if a thing becomes worse, is it not from being better? and if more just, from being more unjust?'

'Of course.'

'Are we satisfied, then,' said Socrates, 'that everything is generated in this way – opposites from opposites?'

'Perfectly.'

'Here is another question. Do not these examples present another feature, that between each pair of opposites there are two processes of generation, one from the first to the second, and another from the second to the first? Between a larger and a smaller object are there not the processes of increase and decrease, and do we not describe them in this way as increasing and decreasing?'

'Yes,' said Cebes.

'Is it not the same with separating and combining, cooling and heating, and all the rest of them? Even if we sometimes do not use the actual terms, must it not in fact hold good universally that they come one from the other, and that there is a process of generation from each to the other?'

'Certainly,' said Cebes.

'Well then,' said Socrates, 'is there an opposite to living, as sleeping is opposite to waking?'

'Certainly.'

'What?'

'Being dead.'

'So if they are opposites, they come from one another, and have their two processes of generation between the two of them?'

'Of course.'

'Very well, then, 'said Socrates, 'I will state one pair of opposites which I mentioned just now; the opposites themselves and the processes between them; and you shall state the other. My opposites are sleeping and waking, and I say that waking comes from sleeping and sleeping from waking, and that the processes between them are going to sleep and waking up. Does that satisfy you,' he asked, 'or not?'

'Perfectly.'

'Now you tell me in the same way,' he went on, 'about life and death. Do you not admit that death is the opposite of life?'

'I do.'

'And that they come from one another?'

'Yes.'

'Then what comes from the living?'

'The dead.'

'And what,' asked Socrates, 'comes from the dead?'

'I must admit,' he said, 'that it is the living.'

'So it is from the dead, Cebes, that living things and people come?'

'Evidently.'

'Then our souls do exist in the next world.'

'So it seems.'

'And one of the two processes in this case is really quite certain – dying is certain enough, isn't it?'

'Yes, it is,' said Cebes.

'What shall we do, then? Shall we omit the complementary process, and leave a defect here in the law of nature? Or must we supply an opposite process to that of dying?'

'Surely we must supply it,' he said.

'And what is it?'

'Coming to life again.'

'Then if there is such a thing as coming to life again,' said Socrates, 'it must be a process from death to life?'

'Quite so.'

'So we agree upon this too: that the living have come from the dead no less than the dead from the living. But I think we decided that if this was so, it was a sufficient proof that the souls of the dead must exist in some place from which they are reborn.'

'It seems to me, Socrates,' he said, 'that this follows necessarily from our agreement.'

'I think there is another way too, Cebes, in which you can see that we were not wrong in our agreement. If there were not a constant correspondence in the process of generation between the two sets of opposites, going round in a sort of cycle; if generation were a straight path to the opposite extreme without any return to the starting-point or any deflection, do you realize that in the end everything would have the same quality and reach the same state, and change would cease altogether?'

'What do you mean?'

'Nothing difficult to understand,' replied Socrates. 'For example, if "falling asleep" existed, and "waking up" did not balance it by making something come out of sleep, you must realize that in the end everything would make Endymion [13] look foolish; he would be nowhere, because the whole world would be in the same state – asleep. And if everything were combined and nothing separated, we should soon have Anaxagoras' "all things together".[14] In just the same way, my dear Cebes, if everything that has some share of life were to die, and if after death the dead remained in that form and did not come to life again, would it not be quite inevitable that in the end everything should be dead and nothing alive? If living things came from other living things, and the living things died, what possible means could prevent their number from being exhausted by death?'

'None that I can see, Socrates,' said Cebes. 'What you say seems to be perfectly true.'

'Yes, Cebes,' he said, 'if anything is true, I believe that this is, and we were not mistaken in our agreement upon it; coming to life again is a fact, and it is a fact that the living come from the dead, and a fact that the souls of the dead exist.'

'Besides, Socrates,' rejoined Cebes, 'there is that theory which you have often described to us – that what we call learning is really just recollection. If that is true, then surely what we recollect now we must have learned at some time before; which is impossible unless our souls existed somewhere before they entered this human shape. So in that way too it seems likely that the soul is immortal.'

'How did the proofs of that theory go, Cebes?' broke

in Simmias. 'Remind me, because at the moment I can't quite remember.'

'One very good argument,' said Cebes, 'is that when people are asked questions, if the question is put in the right way they can give a perfectly correct answer, which they could not possibly do unless they had some knowledge and a proper grasp of the subject. And then if you confront people with a diagram [15] or anything like that, the way in which they react is an unmistakeable proof that the theory is correct.'

'And if you don't find that convincing, Simmias,' said Socrates, 'see whether this appeals to you. I suppose that you find it hard to understand how what we call learning can be recollection?'

'Not at all,' said Simmias. 'All that I want is to be helped to do what we are talking about – to recollect. I can practically remember enough to satisfy me already, from Cebes' approach to the subject; but I should be none the less glad to hear how you meant to approach it.'

'I look at it in this way,' said Socrates. 'We are agreed, I suppose, that if a person is to be reminded of anything, he must first know it at some time or other?'

'Quite so.'

'Are we also agreed in calling it recollection when knowledge comes in a particular way? I will explain what I mean. Suppose that a person on seeing or hearing or otherwise noticing one thing not only becomes conscious of that thing but also thinks of something else which is an object of a different sort of knowledge; are we not justified in saying that he was reminded of the object which he thought of?'

'What do you mean?'

'Let me give you an example. A human being and a musical instrument, I suppose you will agree, are different objects of knowledge.'

'Yes, certainly.'

'Well, you know what happens to lovers when they see a musical instrument or a piece of clothing or any other private property of the person whom they love; when they recognize the thing, their minds conjure up a picture of its owner. That is recollection. In the same way the sight of Simmias often reminds one of Cebes; and of course there are thousands of other examples.'

'Yes, of course there are,' said Simmias.

'So by recollection we mean the sort of experience which I have just described, especially when it happens with reference to things which we had not seen for such a long time that we had forgotten them.'

'Quite so.'

'Well, then, is it possible for a person who sees a picture of a horse or a musical instrument to be reminded of a person, or for someone who sees a picture of Simmias to be reminded of Cebes?'

'Perfectly.'

'And is it possible for someone who sees a portrait of Simmias to be reminded of Simmias himself?'

'Yes, it is.'

'Does it not follow from all this that recollection may be caused either by similar or by dissimilar objects?'

'Yes, it does.'

'When you are reminded by similarity, surely you must also be conscious whether the similarity is perfect or only partial.'

'Yes, you must.'

'Here is a further step,' said Socrates. 'We admit, I suppose, that there is such a thing as equality [16] – not the equality of stick to stick and stone to stone, and so on, but something beyond all that and distinct from it – absolute equality. Are we to admit this or not?'

'Yes indeed,' said Simmias, 'most emphatically.'

'And do we know what it is?'

'Certainly.'

'Where did we get our knowledge? Was it not from

the particular examples that we mentioned just now?
Was it not from seeing equal sticks or stones or other
equal objects that we got the notion of equality, although
it is something quite distinct from them? Look at it in
this way. Is it not true that equal stones and sticks sometimes, without changing in themselves, appear equal to
one person and unequal to another?'

'Certainly.'

'Well, now, have you ever thought that things which
were absolutely equal were unequal, or that equality was
inequality?'

'No, never, Socrates.'

'Then these equal things are not the same as absolute
equality.'

'Not in the least, as I see it, Socrates.'

'And yet it is these equal things that have suggested
and conveyed to you your knowledge of absolute
equality, although they are distinct from it?'

'Perfectly true.'

'Whether it is similar to them or dissimilar?'

'Certainly.'

'It makes no difference,' said Socrates. 'So long as the
sight of one thing suggests another to you, it must be a
cause of recollection, whether the two things are alike
or not.'

'Quite so.'

'Well, now,' he said, 'what do we find in the case of the
equal sticks and other things of which we were speaking
just now: do they seem to us to be equal in the sense of
absolute equality, or do they fall short of it in so far as
they only approximate to equality? Or don't they fall
short at all?'

'They do,' said Simmias, ' a long way.'

'Suppose that when you see something you say to
yourself "This thing which I can see has a tendency to be
like something else, but it falls short and cannot be really
like it, only a poor imitation"; don't you agree with me

123

that anyone who receives that impression must in fact have previous knowledge of that thing which he says that the other resembles, but inadequately?'

'Certainly he must.'

'Very well, then; is that our position with regard to equal things and absolute equality?'

'Exactly.'

'Then we must have had some previous knowledge of equality before the time when we first saw equal things and realized that they were striving after equality, but fell short of it.'

'That is so.'

'And at the same time we are agreed also upon this point, that we have not and could not have acquired this notion of equality except by sight or touch or one of the other senses. I am treating them as being all the same.'

'They are the same, Socrates, for the purpose of our argument.'

'So it must be through the senses that we obtained the notion that all sensible equals are striving after absolute equality but falling short of it. Is that correct?'

'Yes, it is.'

'So before we began to see and hear and use our other senses we must somewhere have acquired the knowledge that there is such a thing as absolute equality; otherwise we could never have realized, by using it as a standard for comparison, that all equal objects of sense are desirous of being like it, but are only imperfect copies.'

'That is the logical conclusion, Socrates.'

'Did we not begin to see and hear and possess our other senses from the moment of birth?'

'Certainly.'

'But we admitted that we must have obtained our knowledge of equality before we obtained them.'

'Yes.'

'So we must have obtained it before birth.'

'So it seems.'

'Then if we obtained it before our birth, and possessed it when we were born, we had knowledge, both before and at the moment of birth, not only of equality and relative magnitudes, but of all absolute standards. Our present argument applies no more to equality than it does to absolute beauty, goodness, uprightness, holiness, and, as I maintain, all those characteristics which we designate in our discussions by the term "absolute". So we must have obtained knowledge of all these characteristics before our birth.'

'That is so.'

'And unless we invariably forget it after obtaining it, we must always be born *knowing* and continue to *know* all through our lives; because "to know" means simply to retain the knowledge which one has acquired, and not to lose it. Is not what we call "forgetting" simply the loss of knowledge, Simmias?'

'Most certainly, Socrates.'

'And if it is true that we acquired our knowledge before our birth, and lost it at the moment of birth, but afterwards, by the exercise of our senses upon sensible objects, recover the knowledge which we had once before, I suppose that what we call learning will be the recovery of our own knowledge; and surely we should be right in calling this recollection.'

'Quite so.'

'Yes, because we saw that it is possible for the perception of an object by sight or hearing or any of the other senses to suggest to the percipient, through association (whether there is any similarity or not) another object which he has forgotten. So, as I maintain, there are two alternatives: either we are all born with knowledge of these standards, and retain it throughout our lives; or else, when we speak of people learning, they are simply recollecting what they knew before; in other words, learning is recollection.'

'Yes, that must be so, Socrates.'

'Which do you choose, then, Simmias? that we are born with knowledge, or that we recollect after we are born the things of which we possessed knowledge before we were born?'

'I don't know which to choose on the spur of the moment, Socrates.'

'Well, here is another choice for you to make. What do you think about this? Can a person who knows a subject thoroughly explain what he knows?'

'Most certainly he can.'

'Do you think that everyone can explain these questions about which we have just been talking?'

'I should like to think so,' said Simmias, 'but I am very much afraid that by this time to-morrow there will be no one on this earth who can do it properly.'

'So you don't think, Simmias, that everyone has knowledge about them?'

'Far from it.'

'Then they just recollect what they once learned.'

'That must be the right answer.'

'When do our souls acquire this knowledge? It cannot be after the beginning of our mortal life.'

'No, of course not.'

'Then it must be before.'

'Yes.'

'Then our souls had a previous existence, Simmias, before they took on this human shape; they were independent of our bodies; and they were possessed of intelligence.'

'Unless perhaps it is at the moment of birth that we acquire knowledge of these things, Socrates; there is still that time available.'

'No doubt, my dear fellow, but just tell me, what other time is there to lose it in? We have just agreed that we do not possess it when we are born. Do we lose it at the same moment that we acquire it? or can you suggest any other time?'

'No, of course not, Socrates; I didn't realize what non-sense I was talking.'

'Well, how do we stand now, Simmias? If all these absolute realities, such as Beauty and Goodness, which we are always talking about, really exist; if it is to them, as we re-discover our own former knowledge of them, that we refer, as copies to their patterns, all the objects of our physical perception; – if these realities exist, does it not follow that our souls must exist too even before our birth, whereas if they do not exist, our discussion would seem to be a waste of time? Is this the position, that it is logically just as certain that our souls exist before our birth as it is that these realities exist, and that if the one is impossible, so is the other?'

'It is perfectly obvious to me, Socrates,' said Simmias, 'that the same logical necessity applies to both. It suits me very well that your argument should rely upon the point that our soul's existence before our birth stands or falls with the existence of your grade of reality. I cannot imagine anything more self-evident than the fact that absolute Beauty and Goodness and all the rest that you mentioned just now exist in the fullest possible sense. In my opinion the proof is quite satisfactory.'

'What about Cebes?' said Socrates. 'We must convince Cebes too.'

'To the best of my belief he is satisfied,' replied Simmias. 'It is true that he is the most obstinate person in the world at resisting an argument, but I should think that he needs nothing more to convince him that our souls existed before our birth. As for their existing after we are dead as well, even I don't feel that that has been proved, Socrates; Cebes' objection still holds: the common fear that a man's soul may be disintegrated at the very moment of his death, and that this may be the end of its existence. Supposing that it *is* born and constituted from some source or other, and exists before it enters a human body: after it has entered one, is there any reason why, at the moment of release, it should not come to an end and be destroyed itself?'

'Quite right, Simmias,' said Cebes. 'It seems that we have got the proof of one half of what we wanted – that the soul existed before birth – but now we need also to prove that it will exist after death no less than before birth, if our proof is to be complete.'

'As a matter of fact, my dear Simmias and Cebes,' said Socrates, 'it is proved already, if you will combine this last argument with the one about which we agreed before, that every living thing comes from the dead. If the soul exists before birth, and if when it proceeds towards life and is born it must be born from death or the dead state, surely it must also exist after death, if it must be born again. So the point which you mention has been proved already. But in spite of this I believe that you and Simmias would like to spin out the discussion still more; you are afraid, as children are, that when the soul emerges from the body the wind may really puff it away and scatter it, especially when a person does not die on a calm day but with a gale blowing.'

Cebes laughed. 'Suppose that we are afraid, Socrates,' he said, 'and try to convince us. Or rather don't suppose that it is we that are afraid; probably even in us there is a little boy who has these childish terrors. Try to persuade him not to be afraid of death as though it were a bogey.'

'What you should do,' said Socrates, 'is to say a magic spell over him every day until you have charmed his fears away.'

'But, Socrates,' said Simmias, 'where shall we find a magician who understands these spells now that you – are leaving us?'

'Greece is a large country, Cebes,' he replied, 'which must have good men in it; and there are many foreign races too. You must ransack all of them in your search for this magician, without sparing money or trouble;

because you could not spend your money more opportunely on any other object. And you must search also by your own united efforts; because it is probable that you would not easily find anyone better fitted for the task.'

'We will see to that,' said Cebes. 'But let us return to the point where we left off, if you have no objection.'

'Of course not; why should I?'

'Thank you,' said Cebes.

'We ought, I think,' said Socrates, 'to ask ourselves this: What sort of thing is it that would naturally suffer the fate of being dispersed? For what sort of thing should we fear this fate, and for what should we not? When we have answered this, we should next consider to which class the soul belongs; and then we shall know whether to feel confidence or fear about the fate of our souls.'

'Quite true.'

'Would you not expect a composite object or a natural compound to be liable to break up where it was put together? and ought not anything which is really incomposite to be the one thing of all others which is not affected in this way?'

'That seems to be the case,' said Cebes.

'Is it not extremely probable that what is always constant and invariable is incomposite, and what is inconstant and variable is composite?'

'That is how it seems to me.'

'Then let us return to the same examples which we were discussing before. Does that absolute Reality which we define in our discussions remain always constant and invariable, or not? Does absolute equality or beauty or any other independent entity which really exists ever admit change of any kind? or does each one of these uniform and independent entities remain always constant and invariable, never admitting any alteration in any respect or in any sense?'

'They must be constant and invariable, Socrates,' said Cebes.

'Well, what about the concrete instances of beauty –
such as men, horses, clothes, and so on – or of equality,
or any other members of a class corresponding to an
absolute entity? Are they constant, or are they, on the
contrary, scarcely ever in the same relation in any sense
either to themselves or to one another?'

'With them, Socrates, it is just the opposite; they are
never free from variation.'

'And these concrete objects you can touch and see and
perceive by your other senses, but those constant entities
you cannot possibly apprehend except by thinking; they
are invisible to our sight.'

'That is perfectly true,' said Cebes.

'So you think that we should assume two classes of
things, one visible and the other invisible?'

'Yes, we should.'

'The invisible being invariable, and the visible never
being the same?'

'Yes, we should assume that too.'

'Well, now,' said Socrates, 'are we not part body, part
soul?'

'Certainly.'

'Then to which class do we say that the body would
have the closer resemblance and relation?'

'Quite obviously to the visible.'

'And the soul, is it visible or invisible?'

'Invisible to men, at any rate, Socrates,' he said.

'But surely we have been speaking of things visible or
invisible to our human nature. Do you think that we had
some other nature in view?'

'No, human nature.'

'What do we say about the soul, then? Is it visible or
invisible?'

'Not visible.'

'Invisible, then?'

'Yes.'

'So soul is more like the invisible, and body more like
the visible?'

'That follows inevitably, Socrates.'

'Did we not say some time ago that when the soul uses the instrumentality of the body for any inquiry, whether through sight or hearing or any other sense (because using the body implies using the senses) it is drawn away by the body into the realm of the variable, and loses its way and becomes confused and dizzy, as though it were fuddled, through contact with things of a similar nature?'

'Certainly.'

'But when it investigates by itself, it passes into the realm of the pure and everlasting and immortal and changeless; and being of a kindred nature, when it is once independent and free from interference, consorts with it always and strays no longer, but remains, in that realm of the absolute, constant and invariable, through contact with beings of a similar nature. And this condition of the soul we call Wisdom.'

'An excellent description, and perfectly true, Socrates.'

'Very well, then; in the light of all that we have said, both now and before, to which class do you think that the soul bears the closer resemblance and relation?'

'I think, Socrates,' said Cebes, 'that even the dullest person would agree, from this line of reasoning, that the soul is in every possible way more like the invariable than the variable.'

'And the body?'

'To the other.'

'Look at it in this way too. When soul and body are both in the same place, nature teaches the one to serve and be subject, the other to rule and govern. In this relation which do you think resembles the divine and which the mortal part? Don't you think that it is the nature of the divine to rule and direct, and that of the mortal to be subject and serve?'

'I do.'

'Then which does the soul resemble?'

'Obviously, Socrates, soul resembles the divine, and body the mortal.'

'Now, Cebes,' he said, 'see whether this is our conclusion from all that we have said. The soul is most like that which is divine, immortal, intelligible, uniform, indissoluble, and ever self-consistent and invariable, whereas body is most like that which is human, mortal, multiform, unintelligible, dissoluble, and never self-consistent. Can we adduce any conflicting argument, my dear Cebes, to show that this is not so?'

'No, we cannot.'

'Very well, then; in that case is it not natural for body to disintegrate rapidly, but for soul to be quite or very nearly indissoluble?'

'Certainly.'

'Of course you know that when a person dies, although it is natural for the visible and physical part of him, which lies here in the visible world and which we call his corpse, to decay and fall to pieces and be dissipated, none of this happens to it immediately; it remains as it was for quite a long time, even if death takes place when the body is well nourished and in the warm season. Indeed, when the body is dried and embalmed, as in Egypt, it remains almost intact for an incredible time; and even if the rest of the body decays, some parts of it – the bones and sinews and anything else like them – are practically everlasting. That is so, is it not?'

'Yes.'

'But the soul, the invisible part, which goes away to a place that is, like itself, glorious, pure, and invisible – the true Hades [17] or unseen world – into the presence of the good and wise God (where, if God so wills, my soul must shortly go) – will it, if its very nature is such as I have described, be dispersed and destroyed at the moment of its release from the body, as is the popular view? Far from it, my dear Simmias and Cebes. The truth is much more like this: If at its release the soul is pure and carries with it no contamination of the body, because it has never willingly associated with it in life, but has shunned it and kept itself separate as its regular practice – in other words, if it has pursued philosophy in the right way and really practised how to face death easily: this is what "practising death" means, isn't it?'

'Most decidedly.'

'Very well; if this is its condition, then it departs to that place which is, like itself, invisible, divine, immortal and wise; where, on its arrival, happiness awaits it, and release from uncertainty and folly, from fears and uncontrolled desires, and all other human evils; and where (as they say of the initiates in the Mysteries) it really spends the rest of time with God. Shall we adopt this view, Cebes, or some other?'

'This one, by all means,' said Cebes.

'But, I suppose, if at the time of its release the soul is tainted and impure, because it has always associated with the body and cared for it and loved it, and has been so beguiled by the body and its passions and pleasures that nothing seems real to it but those physical things which can be touched and seen and eaten and drunk and used for sexual enjoyment; and if it is accustomed to hate and fear and avoid what is invisible and hidden from our eyes, but intelligible and comprehensible by philosophy – if the soul is in this state, do you think that it will escape independent and uncontaminated?'

'That would be quite impossible,' he said.

'On the contrary, it will, I imagine, be permeated by the corporeal, which fellowship and intercourse with the body will have ingrained in its very nature through constant association and long practice.'

'Certainly.'

'And we must suppose, my dear fellow, that the corporeal is heavy, oppressive, earthly and visible. So the soul which is tainted by its presence is weighed down and dragged back into the visible world, through fear (as they say) of Hades or the invisible, and hovers about tombs and graveyards. The shadowy apparitions which have actually been seen there are the ghosts of those souls which have not got clear away, but still retain some portion of the visible; which is why they can be seen.'

'That seems likely enough, Socrates.'

'Yes, it does, Cebes. Of course these are not the souls of the good, but of the wicked, and they are compelled to wander about these places as a punishment for their bad conduct in the past. They continue wandering until at last, through craving for the corporeal, which unceasingly pursues them, they are imprisoned once more in a body. And as you might expect, they are attached to the same sort of character or nature which they have developed during life.'

'What sort do you mean, Socrates?'

'Well, those who have cultivated gluttony or selfishness or drunkenness, instead of taking pains to avoid them, are likely to assume the form of donkeys and other perverse animals; don't you think so?'

'Yes, that is very likely.'

'And those who have deliberately preferred a life of irresponsible lawlessness and violence become wolves and hawks and kites; unless we can suggest any other more likely animals.'

'No, the ones which you mention are exactly right.'

'So it is easy to imagine into what sort of animals all the other kinds of soul will go, in accordance with their conduct during life.'

'Yes, certainly.'

'I suppose that the happiest people, and those who reach the best destination, are the ones who have cultivated the goodness of an ordinary citizen – what is called self-control and integrity – which is acquired by habit and practice, without the help of philosophy and reason.'

'How are these the happiest?'

'Because they will probably pass into some other kind of social and disciplined creature like bees, wasps, and ants; or even back into the human race again, beoming decent citizens.'

'Very likely.'

'But no soul which has not practised philosophy, and is not absolutely pure when it leaves the body, may attain to the divine nature; that is only for the lover of wisdom. This is the reason, my dear Simmias and Cebes, why true philosophers abstain from all bodily desires and withstand them and do not yield to them. It is not because they are afraid of financial loss or poverty, like the average man who thinks of money first; nor because they shrink from dishonour and a bad reputation, like those who are ambitious for distinction and authority.'

'No, those would be unworthy motives, Socrates,' said Cebes.

'They would indeed,' he agreed. 'And so, Cebes, those who care about their souls and do not subordinate them to the body dissociate themselves firmly from these others and refuse to accompany them on their haphazard journey; and, believing that it is wrong to oppose philosophy with her offer of liberation and purification, they turn and follow her wherever she leads.'

'What do you mean, Socrates?'

'I will explain,' he said. 'Every seeker after wisdom knows that up to the time when philosophy takes it over his soul is a helpless prisoner, chained hand and foot in the body, compelled to view reality not directly but only through its prison bars, and wallowing in utter ignorance. And philosophy can see that the imprisonment is ingeniously effected by the prisoner's own active desire, which makes him first accessory to his own confinement. Well, philosophy takes over the soul in this condition and by gentle persuasion tries to set it free. She points out that observation by means of the eyes and ears and all the other senses is entirely deceptive, and she urges the soul to refrain from using them unless it is necessary to do so, and encourages it to collect and concentrate itself by itself, trusting nothing but its own independent judgement upon objects considered in themselves, and attributing no truth to anything which it views indirectly as being subject to variation, because such objects are sensible and visible but what the soul itself sees is intelligible and invisible. Now the soul of the true philosopher feels that it must not reject this opportunity for release, and so it abstains as far as possible from pleasures and desires and griefs, because it reflects that the result of giving way to pleasure or fear or desire is not as might be supposed the trivial misfortune of becoming ill or wasting money through self-indulgence, but the last and worst calamity of all, which the sufferer does not recognize.'

'What is that, Socrates?' asked Cebes.

'When anyone's soul feels a keen pleasure or pain it cannot help supposing that whatever causes the most violent emotion is the plainest and truest reality; which it is not. It is chiefly visible things that have this effect, isn't it?'

'Quite so.'

'Is it not on this sort of occasion that soul passes most completely into the bondage of body?'

'How do you make that out?'

'Because every pleasure or pain has a sort of rivet with which it fastens the soul to the body and pins it down and makes it corporeal, accepting as true whatever the body certifies. The result of agreeing with the body and finding pleasure in the same things is, I imagine, that it cannot help becoming like it in character and training, so that it can never get clean away to the unseen world, but is always saturated with the body when it sets out, and so soon falls back again into another body, where it takes root and grows. Consequently it is excluded from all fellowship with the pure and uniform and divine.'

'Yes, that is perfectly true, Socrates,' said Cebes.

'It is for these reasons, Cebes, that true philosophers

exhibit self-control and courage; not for the reasons which are generally supposed. Or do you think that the popular view is right?'

'No, certainly not.'

'No, indeed. A philosopher's soul will take the view which I have described. It will not first expect to be set free by philosophy, and then allow pleasure and pain to reduce it once more to bondage, thus taking upon itself an endless task, like Penelope [18] when she undid her own weaving; no, this soul secures immunity from its desires by following Reason and abiding always in her company, and by contemplating the true and divine and unconjecturable, and drawing inspiration from it; because such a soul believes that this is the right way to live while life endures, and that after death it reaches a place which is kindred and similar to its own nature, and there is rid for ever of human ills. After such a training, my dear Simmias and Cebes, the soul can have no grounds for fearing that on its separation from the body it will be blown away and scattered by the winds, and so disappear into thin air, and cease to exist altogether.'

There was silence for some time after Socrates had said this. He himself, to judge from his appearance, was still occupied with the argument which he had just been stating, and so were most of us; but Simmias and Cebes went on talking in a low voice. When Socrates noticed them he said 'Why, do you feel that my account is inadequate? Of course it is still open to a number of doubts and objections, if you want to examine it in detail. If it is something else that you two are considering, never mind; but if you feel any difficulty about our discussion, don't hesitate to put forward your own views, and point out any way in which you think that my account could be improved; and by all means make use of my services too, if you think I can help at all to solve the difficulty.'

'Very well, Socrates,' said Simmias, 'I will be quite open with you. We have both been feeling difficulties for some time, and each of us has been urging the other to ask questions. We are anxious to have your answers, but we did not like to bother you, for fear of annoying you in your present misfortune.'

When Socrates heard this he laughed gently and said 'I am surprised at you, Simmias. I shall certainly find it difficult to convince the outside world that I do not regard my present lot as a misfortune if I cannot even convince you, and you are afraid that I am more irritable now than I used to be. Evidently you think that I have less insight into the future than a swan; because when these birds feel that the time has come for them to die, they sing more loudly and sweetly than they have sung in all their lives before, for joy that they are going away into the presence of the god whose servants they are. It is quite wrong for human beings to make out that the swans sing their last song as an expression of grief at their approaching end; people who say this are misled by their own fear of death, and fail to reflect that no bird sings when it is hungry or cold or distressed in any other way; not even the nightingale or swallow or hoopoe, whose song is supposed to be a lament. In my opinion neither they nor the swans sing because they are sad. I believe that the swans, belonging as they do to Apollo, have prophetic powers and sing because they know the good things that await them in the unseen world; and they are happier on that day than they have ever been before. Now I consider that I am in the same service as the swans, and dedicated to the same god; and that I am no worse endowed with prophetic powers by my master than they are, and no more disconsolate at leaving this life. So far as that fear of yours is concerned, you may say and ask whatever you like, so long as the Athenian officers of justice permit.'

'Thank you,' said Simmias. 'I will tell you my difficulty first and then Cebes shall tell you where he finds your theory unacceptable. I think, just as you do,

Socrates, that although it is very difficult if not impossible in this life to achieve certainty about these questions, at the same time it is utterly feeble not to use every effort in testing the available theories, or to leave off before we have considered them in every way, and come to the end of our resources. It is our duty to do one of two things: either to ascertain the facts, whether by seeking instruction or by personal discovery; or, if this is impossible, to select the best and most dependable theory which human intelligence can supply, and use it as a raft to ride the seas of life – that is, assuming that we cannot make our journey with greater confidence and security by the surer means of a divine revelation. And so now, after what you have said, I shall not let any diffidence prevent me from asking my question, and so make me blame myself afterwards for not having spoken my mind now. The fact is, Socrates, that on thinking it over, and discussing it with Cebes here, I feel that your theory has serious flaws in it.'

'Your feeling is very likely right, my dear boy,' said Socrates, 'but tell me where you think the flaws are.'

'What I mean is this,' said Simmias. 'You might say the same thing about tuning the strings of a musical instrument: that the attunement is something invisible and incorporeal and splendid and divine, and located in the tuned instrument, while the instrument itself and its strings are material and corporeal and composite and earthly and closely related to what is mortal. Now suppose that the instrument is broken, or its strings cut or snapped. According to your theory the attunement must still exist – it cannot have been destroyed; because it would be inconceivable that when the strings are broken the instrument and the strings themselves, which have a mortal nature, should still exist, and the attunement, which shares the nature and characteristics of the divine and immortal, should exist no longer, having predeceased its mortal counterpart. You would say that the attunement must still exist somewhere just as it was; and that the wood and strings will rot away before anything happens to it. I say this, Socrates, because, as I think you yourself are aware, we Pythagoreans have a theory of the soul which is roughly like this; the body is held together at a certain tension between the extremes of hot and cold, and dry and wet, and so on, and our soul is a temperament or adjustment of these same extremes, when they are combined in just the right proportion. Well, if the soul is really an adjustment, obviously as soon as the tension of our body is lowered or increased beyond the proper point, the soul must be destroyed, divine though it is; just like any other adjustment, either in music or in any product of the arts and crafts, although in each case the physical remains last considerably longer until they are burnt up or rot away. Find us an answer to this argument, if someone insists that the soul, being a temperament of physical constituents, is the first thing to be destroyed by what we call death.'

Socrates opened his eyes very wide – a favourite trick of his – and smiled. 'Really,' he said, 'Simmias's criticism is quite justified, so if any of you are readier-witted than I am, you had better answer him; it seems to me that he is not handling the argument at all badly. However, before we have the answer, I think we should hear what criticisms Cebes has to make in his turn, so that we may have time to decide what we shall say; when we have heard him, we must either agree with them if they seem to be at all on the right note, or if not, we must then proceed to champion our theory. Come on, Cebes,' he said, 'tell us what has been troubling you.'

'Very well,' said Cebes. 'It seems to me that the argument is just where it was; I mean that it is open to the same criticism that we made before. The proof that our soul existed before it took on this present shape is perfectly satisfying, I might even say convincing; I am not changing my position about that. But as for its still existing somewhere after we are dead, I think that the proof fails in this way. Mind you, I don't agree with Simmias's objection that soul is not stronger and more durable than body; it seems to me to be far superior in every way like that. "Then why", your theory might enquire, "are you still sceptical, when you can see that after a man dies even the weaker part of him continues to exist? Don't you think the more durable part of him must logically survive as long?" Well, here is my answer; I want you to consider whether there is anything in what I say – because like Simmias I must have recourse to an illustration.

'Suppose that an elderly tailor has just died. Your theory would be just like saying that the man is not dead, but still exists somewhere safe and sound; and offering as proof the fact that the coat which he had made for himself and was wearing has not perished but is still intact. If anyone was sceptical, I suppose you would ask him which is likely to last longer, a man or a coat which is being regularly used and worn; and when he replied that the former was far more likely, you would imagine that you had proved conclusively that the man is safe and sound, since the less enduring object has not perished. But surely this is not so, Simmias – because I want your opinion too ; anyone would dismiss such a view as absurd. The tailor makes and wears out any number of coats, but although he outlives all the others, presumably he perishes before the last one; and this does not mean that a man is inferior to a coat, or has a weaker hold upon life. I believe that this analogy might apply to the relation of soul to body; and I think that it would be reasonable to say of them in the same way that soul is a long-lived thing, whereas body is relatively feeble and short-lived. But while we may admit that each soul wears out a number of bodies, especially if it lives a great many years – because although the body is continually changing and disintegrating all through life, the soul never stops replacing what is worn away – still we must suppose that when the soul dies it is still in possession of its latest covering, and perishes before it in this case only; although when the soul has perished the body at last reveals its natural frailty and quickly rots away. If you accept this view there is no justification yet for any confidence that after death our souls still exist somewhere. Suppose that one conceded to the exponent of immortality even more than you claim, granting not only that our souls existed before our birth, but also that some of them may continue to exist or come into existence after death, and be born and die again several times (soul having such natural vitality that it persists through successive incarnations); unless in granting this he made the further concession that the soul suffers no ill effects in its various rebirths, and so does not, at one of its "deaths", perish altogether; if he had to admit that nobody knows which of these "deaths" or separations from the body may prove fatal to the soul (because such insight is impossible for any of us) – on these terms, Socrates, no one but a fool is entitled to face death with confidence, unless he can prove that the soul is absolutely immortal and indestructible. Otherwise everyone must always feel apprehension at the approach of death, for fear that in this particular separation from the body his soul may be finally and utterly destroyed.'

Well, when we had heard them state their objections, we all felt very much depressed, as we told one another later. We had been quite convinced by the earlier part of the discussion, and now we felt that they had upset our convictions and destroyed our confidence not only in what had been said already, but also in anything that was to follow later; perhaps we were incompetent to judge, or the facts themselves might prove to be unreliable.

ECHECRATES: You certainly have my full sympathy, Phaedo. After hearing your account I find myself faced with the same misgiving. How can we believe in anything after this? Socrates' argument was absolutely convincing, and now it is completely discredited. That theory that our soul is a sort of attunement has always had an extraordinary attraction for me, and when I heard it stated it reminded me that I myself had formed the same opinion. What I really need now is another proof, right from the beginning, to convince me that when a man dies his soul does not die with him. Tell me, how did Socrates pick up the trail again? And did he show any sign of being upset, like the rest of you, or did he quietly come to the rescue of the argument? And did he rescue it effectively or not? Tell us every detail as accurately as you can.

PHAEDO: I can assure you, Echecrates, that Socrates often astonished me; but I never admired him more than on this particular occasion. That he should have been ready with an answer was, I suppose, nothing unusual; but what impressed me was first, the pleasant, kindly, appreciative way in which he received the two boys' objections, then his quick recognition of how the turn of the discussion had affected us; and lastly the skill with which he healed our wounds, rallied our scattered forces, and encouraged us to join him in pursuing the inquiry.

ECHECRATES: How did he do that?

PHAEDO: I will tell you. I happened to be sitting to the right of his bed, on a footstool, and he was much higher than I was. So he laid his hand on my head and gathered up the curls on my neck – he never missed a chance of teasing me about my curls – and said 'To-morrow, I suppose, Phaedo, you will cut off this beautiful hair.' [19]

'I expect so, Socrates', I said.

'Not if you take my advice.'

'Why not?' I asked.

'Because I shall cut off mine to-day, and you ought to do the same,' said Socrates, 'that is, if we let our argument die and fail to bring it to life again. What is more, if I were you, and let the truth escape me, I should make a vow like the Argives [20] never to let my hair grow again until I had defeated the argument of Simmias and Cebes in a return battle.'

'But', I objected, 'not even Heracles can take on two at once.'

'You had better call upon me to be your Iolaus,'[21] he said, 'while the daylight lasts.'

'Very well,' I said, 'but I am Iolaus appealing to Heracles, not Heracles to Iolaus.'

'The effect will be just the same,' he said. 'But first there is one danger that we must guard against.'

'What sort of danger?' I asked.

'Of becoming misologic,' he said, 'in the sense that people become misanthropic. No greater misfortune could happen to anyone than that of developing a dislike for argument. Misology and misanthropy arise in just the same way. Misanthropy is induced by believing in somebody quite uncritically. You assume that a person is absolutely truthful and sincere and reliable, and a little later you find that he is shoddy and unreliable. Then the same thing happens again. After repeated disappointments at the hands of the very people who might be supposed to be your nearest and most intimate friends, constant irritation ends by making you dislike everybody and suppose that there is no sincerity to be found anywhere. Have you never noticed this happening?'

'Indeed, I have.'

'Don't you feel that it is reprehensible? Isn't it obvious that such a person is trying to form human relationships without any critical understanding of human nature? Otherwise he would surely recognize the truth: that there are not many very good or very bad people, but the great majority are something between the two.'

'How do you make that out?' I asked.

'On the analogy of very large or small objects,' he said. 'Can you think of anything more unusual than coming across a very large or small man, or dog, or any other creature? or one which is very swift or slow, ugly or beautiful, white or black? Have you never realized that extreme instances are few and rare, while intermediate ones are many and plentiful?'

'Certainly.'

'So you think that if there were a competition in wickedness, very few would distinguish themselves even there?'

'Probably.'

'Yes, it is probable,' said Socrates. 'However, you have led me into a digression. The resemblance between arguments and human beings lies not in what I said just now, but in what I said before: that when one believes that an argument is true without reference to the art of logic, and then a little later decides rightly or wrongly that it is false, and the same thing happens again and again – you know how it is, especially with those who spend their time in arguing both sides; they end by believing that they are wiser than anyone else, because they alone have discovered that there is nothing stable or dependable either in facts or in arguments, and that everything fluctuates just like the water in a tidal channel, and never stays at any point for any time.'

'That is perfectly true,' I said.

'Well, then, Phaedo,' he said, 'supposing that there is an argument which is true and valid and capable of being discovered, if anyone nevertheless, through his experience of these arguments which seem to the same people to be sometimes true and sometimes false, attached no responsibility to himself and his lack of technical ability, but was finally content, in exasperation, to shift the blame from himself to the arguments, and spend the rest of his life loathing and decrying them, and so missed the chance of knowing the truth about reality; would it not be a deplorable thing?'

'It would indeed', I said.

'Very well,' he said, 'that is the first thing that we must

guard against; we must not let it enter our minds that there may be no validity in argument. On the contrary we should recognize that we ourselves are still intellectual invalids; but that we must brace ourselves and do our best to become healthy – you and the others partly with a view to the rest of your lives, but I directly in view of my death; because at the moment I am in danger of regarding it not philosophically but self-assertively. You know how, in an argument, people who have no real education care nothing for the facts of the case, and are only anxious to get their point of view accepted by the audience? Well, I feel that at this present moment I am as bad as they are, only with this difference: that my anxiety will be not to convince my audience (except incidentally) but to produce the strongest possible conviction in myself. This is how I weigh the position, my dear fellow – see how selfish I am! If my theory is really true, it is right to believe it; while, even if death is extinction, at any rate during this time before my death I shall be less likely to distress my companions by giving way to self-pity; and this folly of mine will not live on with me (which would be a calamity) but will shortly come to an end.

'That, my dear Simmias and Cebes, is the spirit in which I am prepared to approach the discussion. As for you, if you will take my advice, you will think very little of Socrates, and much more of the truth. If you think that anything I say is true, you must agree with me; if not, oppose it with every argument that you have. You must not allow me, in my enthusiasm, to deceive both myself and you, and leave my sting behind when I fly away.

'Well, we must go ahead,' he continued. 'First remind me of what you said, if you find my memory inaccurate. Simmias, I believe, is troubled with doubts; he is afraid that, even if the soul is more divine and a higher thing than the body, it may nevertheless be destroyed first, as being a kind of attunement. Cebes on the other hand appeared to agree with me that soul is more enduring than body, but to maintain that no one can be sure that, after repeatedly wearing out a great many bodies, it does not at last perish itself, leaving the last body behind; and he thinks that death may be precisely this, the destruction of the soul, because the body never stops perishing all the time. Am I right, Simmias and Cebes, in thinking that these are the objections which we have to investigate?'

They agreed that this was so.

'Well, then,' he said, 'do you reject all our previous arguments, or only some of them?'

'Only some of them,' they said.

'What is your opinion of the reasoning by which we asserted that learning is recollection, and that, if this is so, our souls must have existed somewhere else before they were confined in the body?'

'Speaking for myself,' said Cebes, 'I found it remarkably convincing at the time, and I stick to it still as I do to no other theory.'

'Yes, indeed,' said Simmias, 'it is just the same with me; I should be very much surprised if I ever changed my opinion about that.'

'But you will have to change it, my Theban friend,' said Socrates, 'if the conception stands that an attunement is a composite thing, and that the soul is an attunement composed of our physical elements at a given tension. I imagine that you would not accept even from yourself the assertion that a composite attunement existed before the elements of which it was to be composed. Or would you?'

'Not for a moment, Socrates.'

'Don't you see that that is just what it amounts to when you say that the soul exists before it enters the human form or body, and also that it is composed of elements which do not yet exist? Surely an attunement is not at all like the object of your comparison. The instrument and the strings and their untuned notes come first; the attunement is the last of all to be constituted and the first to be destroyed. How will this account harmonize with the other?'

'Not at all,' said Simmias.

'And yet,' said Socrates, 'if any account ought to be harmonious, it should be an account of attunement.'

'Yes, it should,' said Simmias.

'Well,' said Socrates, 'this one does not harmonize with your view. Make up your mind which theory you prefer – that learning is recollection, or that soul is an attunement.'

'The former, without any hesitation, Socrates,' he said. 'The other appealed to me, without any proof to support it, as being based on plausible analogy; which is why most people find it attractive. But I realize that theories which rest their proof upon plausibility are impostors, and unless you are on your guard, they deceive you properly, both in geometry and everywhere else. On the other hand, the theory of recollection and learning derives from a hypothesis which is worthy of acceptance. The theory that our soul exists even before it enters the body surely stands or falls with the soul's possession of the ultimate standard of reality; [22] a view which I have, to the best of my belief, fully and rightly accepted. It seems therefore that I must not accept, either from myself or from anyone else, the assertion that soul is an attunement.'

'There is this way of looking at it too, Simmias,' said Socrates. 'Do you think that an attunement, or any other composite thing, should be in a condition different from that of its component elements?'

'No, I do not.'

'And it should not act, or be acted upon, I presume, differently from them?'

He agreed.

'So an attunement should not control its elements, but should follow their lead?'

He assented.

'There is no question of its conflicting with them, either in movement or in sound or in any other way.'

'None at all.'

'Very well then: is it not the nature of every attunement to be an attunement in so far as it is tuned?'

'I don't understand.'

'Surely,' said Socrates, 'if it is tuned more, that is, in a greater degree (supposing this to be possible) it must be more of an attunement; and if it is tuned less, that is, in a lesser degree, it must be less of an attunement.'

'Quite so.'

'And is this the case with the soul – that one soul is, even minutely, more or less of a soul than another?'

'Not in the least.'

'Now please give me your closest attention,' said Socrates. 'Do we say that one kind of soul possesses intelligence and goodness, and is good, and that another possesses stupidity and wickedness, and is evil? And is this true?'

'Yes, it is true.'

'Then how will a person who holds that the soul is an attunement account for the presence in it of goodness and badness? Will he describe them as yet another attunement or lack of it? Will he say that the good soul is in tune, and not only is an attunement itself, but contains another, whereas the bad soul is out of tune and does not contain another attunement?'

'I really could not say,' replied Simmias; 'but obviously anyone who held that view would have to say something of the sort.'

'But we have already agreed', said Socrates, 'that no soul can be more or less of a soul than another; and this is the same as agreeing that no attunement can be more of an attunement and in a greater degree, or less of an attunement and in a lesser degree, than another. Is that not so?'

'Certainly.'

'And that what is neither more nor less of an attunement is neither more nor less in tune. Is that so?'

'Yes.'

'Does that which is neither more nor less in tune contain a greater or smaller proportion of attunement, or an equal one?'

'An equal one.'

'Then since no soul is any more or less than just a soul, it is neither more nor less in tune.'

'That is so.'

'Under this condition it cannot contain a greater proportion of discord or attunement.'

'Certainly not.'

'And again under this condition can one soul contain a greater proportion of badness or goodness than another, assuming that badness is discord and goodness attunement?'

'No, it cannot.'

'Or rather, I suppose, Simmias, by strict reasoning no soul will contain any share of badness, if it is an attunement; because surely since attunement is absolutely attunement and nothing else, it can never contain any share of discord.'

'No, indeed.'

'Nor can the soul, since it is absolutely soul, contain a share of badness.'

'Not in the light of what we have said.'

'So on this theory every soul of every living creature will be equally good – assuming that it is the nature of all souls to be equally souls and nothing else.'

'I think that follows, Socrates.'

'Do you also think that this view is right? Would the argument ever have come to this if our hypothesis, that the soul is an attunement, had been correct?'

'Not the least chance of it.'

'Well,' said Socrates, 'do you hold that it is any other part of a man than the soul that governs him, especially if it is a wise one?'

'No, I do not.'

'Does it yield to the feelings of the body, or oppose them? I mean, for instance, that when a person is feverish and thirsty it impels him the other way, not to drink; and when he is hungry, not to eat; and there are thousands of other ways in which we see the soul opposing the physical instincts. Is that not so?'

'Certainly.'

'Did we not also agree a little while ago that if it is an attunement it can never sound a note that conflicts with the tension or relaxation or vibration or any other condition of its constituents, but must always follow them and never direct them?'

'Yes, we did, of course.'

'Well, surely we can see now that the soul works in just the opposite way. It directs all the elements of which it is said to consist, opposing them in almost everything all through life, and exercising every form of control; sometimes by severe and unpleasant methods like those of physical training and medicine, and sometimes by milder ones; sometimes scolding, sometimes encouraging; and conversing with the desires and passions and fears as though it were quite separate and distinct from them. It is just like Homer's description in the Odyssey [23] where he says that Odysseus

> Then beat his breast, and thus reproved his heart:
> "Endure, my heart; still worse hast thou endured."

Do you suppose that when he wrote that he thought that the soul was an attunement, liable to be swayed by physical feelings? Surely he regarded it as capable of swaying and controlling them; as something much too divine to rank as an attunement.'

'That is certainly how it seems to me, Socrates.'

'Good. In that case there is no justification for our saying that soul is a kind of attunement. We should neither agree with Homer nor be consistent ourselves.'

'That is so.'

'Well now,' said Socrates, 'we seem to have placated the Theban lady Harmonia [24] with moderate success. But what about Cadmus, Cebes? How shall we placate him, and what argument shall we use?'

'I think that you will find a way,' said Cebes. 'This argument which you brought forward against the attunement theory far surpassed all my expectations. When Simmias was explaining his difficulties I wondered very much whether anyone would be able to do anything with his argument; so I was quite astonished that it could not stand up against your very first attack. I should not be surprised if Cadmus' argument met the same fate.'

'My dear fellow,' said Socrates, 'don't boast, or some misfortune will upset the forthcoming argument. However, we will leave that to God; it is our task to come to close quarters in the Homeric manner and test the validity of your contention.

'What you require, in a nutshell, is this. You consider that, unless the confidence of a philosopher who at the point of dying believes that after death he will be better off for having lived and ended his life in philosophy than in any other way of living is to be a blind and foolish confidence, the soul must be proved to be indestructible and immortal. To show that it has great vitality and a godlike nature, and even that it existed before we were born – all this, you say, may very well indicate not that the soul is immortal, but merely that it is long-lived, and pre-existed somewhere for a prodigious period of time, enjoying a great measure of knowledge and activity. But all this did not make it any the more immortal, indeed its very entrance into the human body was, like a disease, the beginning of its destruction; it lives this life in increasing weariness, and finally perishes in what we call death. You also say that, to our individual fears, it makes no difference whether it enters the body once or often; anyone who does not know and cannot prove that the soul is immortal must be afraid, unless he is a fool.

'That, I believe, is the substance of your objection, Cebes. I am deliberately reviewing it more than once, in order that nothing may escape us, and that you may add to it or subtract from it anything that you wish.'

Cebes said 'But at the present moment there is no need for me to add or subtract anything; that is precisely my point of view.'

After spending some time in reflection Socrates said 'What you require is no light undertaking, Cebes. It involves a full treatment of the causes of generation and destruction. If you like, I will describe my own experiences in this connexion; and then, if you find anything helpful in my account, you can use it to reassure yourself about your own objections.'

'Yes, indeed,' said Cebes, 'I should like that very much.'

'Then listen, and I will tell you. When I was young,[25] Cebes, I had an extraordinary passion for that branch of learning which is called natural science; I thought it would be marvellous to know the causes for which each thing comes and ceases and continues to be. I was constantly veering to and fro, puzzling primarily over this sort of question "Is it when heat and cold produce fermentation, as some have said, that living creatures are bred? Is it with the blood that we think, or with the air or the fire that is in us? Or is it none of these, but the brain that supplies our senses of hearing and sight and smell; and from these that memory and opinion arise, and from memory and opinion, when established, that knowledge comes?" Then again I would consider how these faculties are lost, and study celestial and terrestrial

phenomena, until at last I came to the conclusion that I
was uniquely unfitted for this form of inquiry. I will give
you a sufficient indication of what I mean. I had understood some things plainly before, in my own and other
people's estimation; but now I was so befogged by these
speculations that I unlearned even what I had thought I
knew, especially about the cause of growth [26] in human
beings. Previously I had thought that it was quite obviously due to eating and drinking; that when, from the
food which we consume, flesh is added to flesh and bone
to bone, and when in the same way the other parts of the
body are augmented by their appropriate particles, the
bulk which was small is now large; and in this way the
small man becomes a big one. That is what I used to
believe; reasonably, don't you think?'

'Yes, I do,' said Cebes.

'Consider a little further. I had been content to think,
when I saw a tall man standing beside a short one, that
he was taller by a head [27]; and similarly in the case of
horses. And it seemed to me even more obvious that ten
is more than eight because it contains two more; and
that two feet is bigger than one because it exceeds it by
half its own length.'

'And what do you believe about them now?' asked
Cebes.

'Why, upon my word, that I am very far from supposing that I know the explanation of any of these things.
I cannot even convince myself that when you add one to
one either the first or the second one becomes two, or
they both become two by the addition [28] of the one to the
other. I find it hard to believe that, although when they
were separate each of them was one and they were not
two, now that they have come together the cause of their
becoming two is simply the union caused by their juxta-
position. Nor can I believe now, when you divide one,
that this time the cause of its becoming two is the division; because this cause of its becoming two is the oppo-

site of the former one: then it was because they were brought close together and added one to the other, but now it is because they are taken apart and separated one from the other. Nor can I now persuade myself that I understand how it is that things become one; nor, in short, why anything else comes or ceases or continues to be, according to this method of inquiry. So I reject it altogether, and muddle out a haphazard method of my own.

'However, I once heard someone reading from a book (as he said) by Anaxagoras, and asserting that it is Mind that produces order and is the cause of everything. This explanation pleased me.[29] Somehow it seemed right that Mind should be the cause of everything; and I reflected that if this is so, Mind in producing order sets everything in order and arranges each individual thing in the way that is best for it. Therefore if anyone wished to discover the reason why any given thing came or ceased or continued to be, he must find out how it was best for that thing to be, or to act or be acted upon in any other way. On this view there was only one thing for a man to consider, with regard both to himself and to anything else, namely the best and highest good; although this would necessarily imply knowing what is less good, since both were covered by the same knowledge.

'These reflections made me suppose, to my delight, that in Anaxagoras I had found an authority on causation who was after my own heart. I assumed that he would begin by informing us whether the earth is flat or round,[30] and would then proceed to explain in detail the reason and logical necessity for this by stating how and why it was better that it should be so. I thought that if he asserted that the earth was in the centre,[31] he would explain in detail that it was better for it to be there; and if he made this clear, I was prepared to give up hankering after any other kind of cause. I was prepared also in the same way to receive instruction about the sun and moon and the other heavenly bodies, about their relative velocities and their orbits [32] and all the other phenomena connected with them – in what way it is better for each one of them to act or be acted upon as it is. It never entered my head that a man who asserted that the ordering of things is due to Mind would offer any other explanation for them than that it is best for them to be as they are. I thought that by assigning a cause to each phenomenon separately and to the universe as a whole he would make perfectly clear what is best for each and what is the universal good. I would not have parted with my hopes for a great sum of money. I lost no time in procuring the books, and began to read them as quickly as I possibly could, so that I might know as soon as possible about the Best and the Less Good.

'It was a wonderful hope, my friend, but it was quickly dashed. As I read on I discovered that the fellow made no use of Mind and assigned to it no causality for the order of the world, but adduced causes like air and ether and water and many other absurdities. It seemed to me that he was just about as inconsistent as if someone were to say "The cause of everything that Socrates does is Mind" and then, in trying to account for my several actions, said first that the reason why I am lying here now is that my body is composed of bones and sinews, and that the bones are rigid and separated at the joints, but the sinews are capable of contraction and relaxation, and form an envelope for the bones with the help of the flesh and skin, the latter holding all together; and since the bones move freely in their joints the sinews by relaxing and contracting enable me somehow to bend my limbs; and that is the cause of my sitting here in a bent position. Or again, if he tried to account in the same way for my conversing with you, adducing causes such as sound and air and hearing and a thousand others, and never troubled to mention the real reasons; which are that since Athens has thought it better to condemn me, therefore I for my part have thought it better to sit here, and more right to stay and submit to whatever penalty she orders – because, by Dog! I fancy that these sinews and bones would have been in the neighbourhood of Megara or Boeotia long ago (impelled by a conviction of what is best!) if I did not think that it was more right and honourable to submit to whatever penalty my country orders rather than take to my heels and run away. But to call things like that causes is too absurd. If it were said that without such bones and sinews and all the rest of them I should not be able to do what I think is right, it would be true; but to say that it is because of them that I do what I am doing, and not through choice of what is best – although my actions are controlled by Mind – would be a very lax and inaccurate form of expression. Fancy being unable to distinguish between the cause of a thing, and the condition without which it could not be a cause! It is this latter, as it seems to me, that most people, groping in the dark, call a cause – attaching to it a name to which it has no right. That is why one person surrounds the earth with a vortex, and so keeps it in place by means of the heavens; and another props it up on a pedestal of air,[33] as though it were a wide platter. As for a power which keeps things disposed at any given moment in the best possible way, they neither look for it nor believe that it has any supernatural force; they imagine that they will some day find a more mighty and immortal and all-sustaining Atlas; and they do not think that anything is really bound and held together by goodness or moral obligation. For my part, I should be delighted to learn about the workings of such a cause from anyone, but since I have been denied knowledge of it, and have been unable either to discover it myself or to learn about it from another, I have worked out my own makeshift approach to the problem of causation. Would you like me to give you a demonstration of it, Cebes?'

'I should like it very much indeed.'

'Well, after this,' said Socrates, 'when I was worn out with my physical investigations, it occurred to me that I must guard against the same sort of risk which people run when they watch and study an eclipse of the sun; they really do sometimes injure their eyes, unless they study its reflection in water or some other medium. I conceived of something like this happening to myself, and I was afraid that by observing objects with my eyes and trying to comprehend them with each of my other senses I might blind my soul altogether. So I decided that I must have recourse to theories, and use them in trying to discover the truth about things. Perhaps my illustration is not quite apt; because I do not at all admit that an inquiry by means of theory employs "images" any more than one which confines itself to facts. But however that may be, I started off in this way; and in every case I first lay down the theory which I judge to be soundest; and then whatever seems to agree with it – with regard either to causes or to anything else – I assume to be true, and whatever does not I assume not to be true. But I should like to express my meaning more clearly; because at present I don't think that you understand.'

'No, indeed I don't,' said Cebes, 'not a bit.'

'Well,' said Socrates, 'what I mean is this, and there is nothing new about it; I have always said it, in fact I have never stopped saying it, especially in the earlier part of this discussion. As I am going to try to explain to you the theory of causation which I have worked out myself, I propose to make a fresh start from those principles [34] of mine which you know so well; that is, I am assuming the existence of absolute Beauty and Goodness and Magnitude and all the rest of them. If you grant my assumption and admit that they exist, I hope with their help to explain causation to you, and to find a proof that soul is immortal.'

'Certainly I grant it,' said Cebes; 'you need lose no time in drawing your conclusion.'

'Then consider the next step, and see whether you share my opinion. It seems to me that whatever else is beautiful apart from absolute Beauty is beautiful because it partakes of that absolute Beauty, and for no other reason. Do you accept this kind of causality?'

'Yes, I do.'

'Well, now, that is as far as my mind goes; I cannot understand these other ingenious theories of causation. If someone tells me that the reason why a given object is beautiful is that it has a gorgeous colour or shape or any other such attribute, I disregard all these other explanations – I find them all confusing – and I cling simply and straightforwardly and no doubt foolishly to the explanation that the one thing that makes that object beautiful is the presence in it or association with it (in whatever way the relation comes about) of absolute Beauty. I do not go so far as to insist upon the precise details; only upon the fact that it is by Beauty that beautiful things are beautiful. This, I feel, is the safest answer for me or for anyone else to give, and I believe that while I hold fast to this I cannot fall; it is safe for me or for anyone else to answer that it is by Beauty that beautiful things are beautiful. Don't you agree?'

'Yes, I do.'

'Then is it also by largeness that large things are large and larger things larger, and by smallness that smaller things are smaller?'

'Yes.'

'So you too, like myself, would refuse to accept the statement that one man is taller than another "by a head",[35] and that the shorter man is shorter by the same; you would protest that the only view which you yourself can hold is that whatever is taller than something else is so simply by tallness – that is, because of tallness; and that what is shorter is so simply by shortness, that is, because of shortness. You would be afraid, I suppose, that if you said that one man is taller than another by a

head, you would be faced by a logical objection: first that
the taller should be taller and the shorter shorter by the
same thing, and secondly that the taller person should be
taller by a head, which is a short thing, and that it is unnatural that a man should be made tall by something
short. Isn't that so?'

Cebes laughed and said 'Yes, it is.'

'Then you would be afraid to say that ten is more than
eight "by two", or that two is the cause of its excess over
eight, instead of saying that it is more than eight by, or
because of, being a larger number; and you would be
afraid to say that a length of two feet is greater than one
foot by a half, instead of saying that it is greater by its
larger size? – because there is the same danger here too.'

'Quite so.'

'Suppose next that we add one to one; you would
surely avoid saying that the cause of our getting two is
the addition, or in the case of a divided unit, the division.
You would loudly proclaim that you know of no other
way in which any given object can come into being
except by participation in the reality peculiar to its appropriate universal; and that in the cases which I have mentioned you recognize no other cause for the coming into
being of two than participation in duality; and that whatever is to become two must participate in this, and whatever is to become one must participate in unity. You
would dismiss these divisions and additions and other
such niceties, leaving them for persons wiser than yourself to use in their explanations, while you, being nervous
of your own shadow, as the saying is, and of your inex-
perience, would hold fast to the security of your hypothesis and make your answers accordingly. If anyone
should fasten upon the hypothesis itself, you would disregard him and refuse to answer until you could consider whether its consequences were mutually consistent
or not. And when you had to substantiate the hypothesis
itself, you would proceed in the same way, assuming

whatever more ultimate hypothesis commended itself
most to you, until you reached one which was satisfactory. You would not mix the two things together by discussing both the principle and its consequences, like one
of these destructive critics [36] – that is, if you wanted to
discover any part of the truth. They presumably have no
concern or care whatever for such an object, because
their cleverness enables them to muddle everything up
without disturbing their own self-complacence; but you,
I imagine, if you are a philosopher, will follow the
course which I describe.'

'You are perfectly right,' said Simmias and Cebes together.

ECHECRATES: I can assure you, Phaedo, I am not surprised. It seems to me that Socrates made his meaning
extraordinarily clear to even a limited intelligence.

PHAEDO: That was certainly the feeling of all of us who
were present, Echecrates.

ECHECRATES: No doubt, because it is just the same with
us who were not present and are hearing it now for the
first time. But how did the discussion go on?

PHAEDO: I think that when Socrates had got this accepted,
and it was agreed that the various Forms exist, and that
the reason why other things are called after the Forms is
that they participate in the Forms, he next went on to
ask 'If you hold this view, I suppose that when you say
that Simmias is taller than Socrates but shorter than
Phaedo, you mean that at that moment there are in
Simmias both tallness and shortness [37]?'

'Yes, I do.'

'But do you agree that the statement "Simmias is bigger than Socrates" is not true in the form in which it is
expressed? Surely the real reason why Simmias is bigger
is not because he is Simmias but because of the height
which he incidentally possesses; and conversely the
reason why he is bigger than Socrates is not because
Socrates is Socrates, but because Socrates has the attri-

bute of shortness in comparison with Simmias' height.'

'True.'

'And again Simmias' being smaller than Phaedo is due not to the fact that Phaedo is Phaedo, but to the fact that Phaedo has the attribute of tallness in comparison with Simmias' shortness.'

'Quite so.'

'So that is how Simmias comes to be described as both short and tall, because he is intermediate between the two of them, and allows his shortness to be surpassed by the tallness of the one while he asserts his superior tallness over the shortness of the other.' He added with a smile 'I seem to be developing an artificial style [38]; but the facts are surely as I say.'

Simmias agreed.

'I am saying all this because I want you to share my point of view. It seems to me not only that the Form of tallness itself absolutely declines [39] to be short as well as tall, but also that the tallness which is in us never admits smallness and declines to be surpassed. It does one of two things: either it gives way and withdraws as its opposite shortness approaches, or it has already ceased to exist by the time that the other arrives. It cannot stand its ground and receive the quality of shortness in the same way as I myself have done. [40] If it did, it would become different from what it was before, whereas I have not lost my identity by acquiring the quality of shortness; I am the same man, only short; but my tallness could not endure to be short instead of tall. In the same way the shortness that is in us declines ever to become or be tall; nor will any other quality, while still remaining what it was, at the same time become or be the opposite quality; in such a situation it either withdraws or ceases to exist.'

'I agree with you entirely,' said Cebes.

At this point [41] one of the company – I can't remember distinctly who it was – said 'Look here! Didn't we agree, earlier in the discussion, on the exact opposite of what you are saying now: that the bigger comes from the smaller and the smaller from the bigger, and that it is precisely from their opposites that opposites come? Now the view seems to be that this is impossible.'

Socrates had listened with his head turned towards the speaker. 'It was brave of you to refresh my memory,' he said 'but you don't realize the difference between what we are saying now and what we said then. Then we were saying that opposite *things* come from opposite *things*; now we are saying that the opposite *itself* can never become opposite to *itself* – neither the opposite which is in us nor that which is in the real world. Then, my friend, we were speaking about objects which possess opposite qualities, and calling them by the names of the latter; but now we are speaking about the qualities themselves, from whose presence in them the objects which are called after them derive their names. We maintain that the opposites themselves would absolutely refuse to tolerate coming into being from one another.' As he spoke he looked at Cebes. 'I suppose that nothing in what he said worried you too, Cebes?'

'No, not this time,' said Cebes, 'though I don't deny that a good many other things do.'

'So we are agreed upon this as a general principle: that an opposite can never be opposite to itself.'

'Absolutely.'

'Then consider this point too, and see whether you agree about it too. Do you admit that there are such things as heat and cold?'

'Yes, I do.'

'Do you think they are the same as snow and fire?'

'Certainly not.'

'Heat is quite distinct from fire, and cold from snow?'

'Yes.'

'But I suppose you agree, in the light of what we said before, that snow, being what it is, can never admit heat and still remain snow, just as it was before, only with the addition of heat. It must either withdraw at the approach of heat, or cease to exist.'

'Quite so.'

'Again, fire must either retire or cease to exist at the approach of cold. It will never have the courage to admit cold and still remain fire, just as it was, only with the addition of cold.'

'That is true.'

'So we find, in certain cases like these, that the name of the Form is eternally applicable not only to the Form itself, but also to something else, which is not the Form but invariably possesses its distinguishing characteristic. But perhaps another example will make my meaning clearer. Oddness must always be entitled to this name by which I am now calling it; isn't that so?'

'Certainly.'

'This is the question: Is it unique in this respect, or is there something else, not identical with Oddness, to which we are bound always to apply not only its own name but that of Odd as well, because by its very nature it never loses its oddness? What I mean is illustrated by the case of the number Three; there are plenty of other examples, but take the case of Three. Don't you think that it must always be described not only by its own name but by that of Odd, although Odd and Three are not the same thing? It is the very nature of Three and Five and all the alternate integers that every one of them is invariably Odd, although it is not identical with Oddness. Similarly two and four and all the rest of the other series are not identical with Even, but each one of them always *is* even. Do you admit this, or not?'

'Of course I do.'

'Well, then, pay careful attention to the point which I want to make, which is this. It seems clear that the opposites themselves do not admit one another; but it also looks as though any things which, though not themselves opposites, always have opposites in them, similarly do not admit the opposite Form to that which is in them, but on its approach either cease to exist or retire before it. Surely we must assert that Three will sooner cease to exist or suffer any other fate than submit to become Even while it is still Three?'

'Certainly,' said Cebes.

'And yet Two and Three [42] are not opposites.'

'No, they are not.'

'So it is not only the opposite Forms that cannot face one another's approach; there are other things too which cannot face the approach of opposites.'

'That is quite true.'

'Shall we try, if we can, to define what sort of things these are?'

'By all means.'

'Well, then, Cebes, would this describe them – that they are things which are compelled by some Form which takes possession of them to assume not only its own form but invariably also that of some other Form which is an opposite?'

'What do you mean?'

'Just what we were saying a minute ago. You realize, I suppose, that when the Form of Three takes possession of any group of objects, it compels them to be odd as well as three.'

'Certainly.'

'Then I maintain that into such a group the opposite Form to the one which has this effect can never enter.'

'No, it cannot.'

'And it was the Form of Odd that had this effect?'

'Yes.'

'And the opposite of this is the Form of Even?'

'Yes.'

'So the Form of Even will never enter into Three.'

'No, never.'

'In other words, three is incompatible with evenness.'

PLATO

'Quite.'

'So the number three is uneven.' [43]

'Yes.'

'I proposed just now to define what sort of things they are which, although they are not themselves directly opposed to a given opposite, nevertheless do not admit it; as in the present example, Three, although not the opposite of Even, nevertheless does not admit it, because Three is always accompanied by the opposite of Even; and similarly with Two and Odd, or Fire and Cold, and hosts of others. Well, see whether you accept this definition: Not only does an opposite not admit its opposite, but if anything is accompanied by a Form which has an opposite, and meets that opposite, then the thing which is accompanied never admits the opposite of the Form by which it is accompanied. Let me refresh your memory; there is no harm in hearing a thing several times. Five will not admit the Form of Even, nor will ten, which is double five, admit the Form of Odd. Double has an opposite of its own, but at the same time it will not admit the Form of Odd. Nor will one and a half, or other fractions such as a half or three-quarters and so on, admit the Form of Whole. I assume that you follow me and agree.'

'I follow and agree perfectly,' said Cebes.

'Then run over the same ground with me from the beginning; and don't answer in the exact terms [44] of the question, but follow my example. I say this because besides the "safe answer" that I described at first, as the result of this discussion I now see another means of safety. Suppose, for instance, that you ask me what must be present in body to make it hot, I shall not return the safe but ingenuous answer that it is heat, but a more sophisticated one, based on the results of our discussion – namely that it is fire. And if you ask what must be present in a body to make it diseased, I shall say not disease but fever. Similarly if you ask what must be present in a number to make it odd, I shall say not oddness but unity; and so on. See whether you have a sufficient grasp now of what I want from you.'

'Quite sufficient.'

'Then tell me, what must be present in a body to make it alive?'

'Soul.'

'Is this always so?'

'Of course.'

'So whenever soul takes possession of a body, it always brings life with it?'

'Yes, it does.'

'Is there an opposite to life, or not?'

'Yes, there is.'

'What?'

'Death.'

'Does it follow, then, from our earlier agreement, that soul will never admit the opposite of that which accompanies it?'

'Most definitely,' said Cebes.

'Well, now, what name did we apply just now to that which does not admit the Form of even?'

'Uneven.'

'And what do we call that which does not admit justice, or culture?'

'Uncultured; and the other unjust.'

'Very good. And what do we call that which does not admit death?'

'Immortal.' [45]

'And soul does not admit death?'

'No.'

'So soul is immortal.'

'Yes, it is immortal.'

'Well,' said Socrates, 'can we say that that has been proved? What do you think?'

'Most completely, Socrates.'

'Here is another question for you, Cebes. If the uneven

were necessarily imperishable, would not three be imperishable?'

'Of course.'

'Then again, if what is not hot were necessarily imperishable, when you applied heat to snow, would not the snow withdraw still intact and unmelted? It could not cease to exist, nor on the other hand could it remain where it was and admit the heat.'

'That is true.'

'In the same way I assume that if what is not cold were imperishable, when anything cold approached fire, it could never go out or cease to exist; it would depart and be gone unharmed.'

'That must be so.'

'Are we not bound to say the same of the immortal? If what is immortal is also imperishable, it is impossible that at the approach of death soul should cease to be. It follows from what we have already said that it cannot admit death, or be dead; just as we said that three cannot be even, nor can odd; nor can fire be cold, nor can the heat which is in the fire. "But", it may be objected, "granting (as has been agreed) that odd does not become even at the approach of even, why should it not cease to exist, and something even take its place?" In reply to this we could not insist that the odd does not cease to exist – because what is not even is not imperishable; but if this were conceded, we could easily insist that, at the approach of even, odd and three retire and depart. And we could be equally insistent about fire and heat and all the rest of them, could we not?'

'Certainly.'

'So now in the case of the immortal, if it is conceded that this is also imperishable, soul will be imperishable as well as immortal. Otherwise we shall need another argument.'

'There is no need on that account,' said Cebes. 'If what is immortal and eternal cannot avoid destruction, it is hard to see how anything else can.'

'And I imagine that it would be admitted by everyone', said Socrates, 'that God at any rate, and the Form of life, and anything else that is immortal, can never cease to exist.'

'Yes indeed; by all men certainly, and even more, I suppose, by the gods.'

'Then since what is immortal is also indestructible, if soul is really immortal, surely it must be imperishable too.'

'Quite inevitably.'

'So it appears that when death comes to a man, the mortal part of him dies, but the immortal part retires at the approach of death and escapes unharmed and indestructible.'

'Evidently.'

'Then it is as certain as anything can be, Cebes, that soul is immortal and imperishable, and that our souls will really exist in the next world.'

'Well, Socrates,' said Cebes, 'for my part I have no criticisms, and no doubt about the truth of your argument. But if Simmias here or anyone else has any criticism to make, he had better not keep it to himself; because if anyone wants to say or hear any more about this subject, I don't see to what other occasion he is to defer it.'

'As a matter of fact,' said Simmias, 'I have no doubts myself either now, in view of what you have just been saying. All the same, the subject is so vast, and I have such a poor opinion of our weak human nature, that I can't help still feeling some misgivings.'

'Quite right, Simmias,' said Socrates, 'and what is more, even if you find our original assumptions convincing, they still need more accurate consideration. If you and your friends examine them closely enough, I believe that you will arrive at the truth of the matter, in so far as it is possible for the human mind to attain it; and if you are sure that you have done this, you will not need to inquire further.'

'That is true,' said Simmias.

'But there is a further point, gentlemen,' said Socrates, 'which deserves your attention. If the soul is immortal, it demands our care not only for that part of time which we call life, but for all time; and indeed it would seem now that it will be extremely dangerous to neglect it. If death were a release from everything, it would be a boon for the wicked, because by dying they would be released not only from the body but also from their own wickedness together with the soul; but as it is, since the soul is clearly immortal, it can have no escape or security from evil except by becoming as good and wise as it possibly can. For it takes nothing with it to the next world except its education and training; and these, we are told,[46] are of supreme importance in helping or harming the newly dead at the very beginning of his journey there.

'This is how the story goes. When any man dies, his own guardian spirit, which was given charge over him in his life, tries [47] to bring him to a certain place where all must assemble, and from which, after submitting their several cases to judgement, they must set out for the next world, under the guidance of one who has the office of escorting souls from this world to the other. When they have there undergone the necessary experiences and remained as long as is required, another guide brings them back again after many vast periods of time.

'Of course this journey is not as Aeschylus [48] makes Telephus describe it. He says that the path to Hades is straightforward, but it seems clear to me that it is neither straightforward nor single. If it were, there would be no need for a guide, because surely nobody could lose his way anywhere if there were only one road. In fact, it seems likely that it contains many forkings and cross-roads, to judge from the ceremonies [49] and observances of this world.

'Well, the wise and disciplined soul follows its guide

and is not ignorant of its surroundings, but the soul which is deeply attached to the body, as I said before,[50] hovers round it and the visible world for a long time, and it is only after much resistance and suffering that it is at last forcibly led away by its appointed guardian spirit. And when it reaches the same place as the rest, the soul which is impure through having done some impure deed, either by setting its hand to lawless bloodshed or by committing other kindred crimes which are the work of kindred souls, this soul is shunned and avoided by all; none will company with it or guide it; and it wanders alone in utter desolation until certain times have passed, whereupon it is borne away of necessity to its proper habitation. But every soul that has lived throughout its life in purity and soberness enjoys divine company and guidance, and each inhabits the place which is proper to it. There are many wonderful regions in the earth; and the earth itself is neither in nature nor in size such as geographers suppose it to be; so someone [51] has assured me.'

'How can you say that, Socrates?' said Simmias. 'I myself have heard a great many theories about the earth, but not this belief of yours. I should very much like to hear it.'

'Why, really, Simmias, I don't think that it calls for the skill of a Glaucus [52] to explain what my belief is; but to prove that it is true seems to me to be too difficult even for a Glaucus. In the first place I should probably be unable to do it; and in the second, even if I knew how, it seems to me, Simmias, that my life is too short for a long explanation. However, there is no reason why I should not tell you what I believe about the appearance of the earth and regions in it.'

'Well,' said Simmias, 'even that will do.'

'This is what I believe, then,' said Socrates. 'In the first place, if the earth is spherical and in the middle of the heavens, it needs neither air nor any other such force to keep it from falling; the uniformity of the heavens and the equilibrium of the earth itself are sufficient to support it. Any body in equilibrium, if it is set in the middle of a uniform medium, will have no tendency to sink or rise in any direction more than another, and having equal impulses will remain suspended. This is the first article of my belief.'

'And quite right too,' said Simmias.

'Next,' said Socrates, 'I believe that it is vast in size, and that we who dwell between the river Phasis [53] and the Pillars of Hercules inhabit only a minute portion of it; we live round the sea like ants or frogs round a pond; and there are many other peoples inhabiting similar regions. There are many hollow places all round the earth, places of every shape and size, into which the water and mist and air have collected. But the earth itself is as pure as the starry heaven in which it lies, and which is called Ether by most of our authorities. The water, mist, and air are the dregs of this Ether, and they are continually draining into the hollow places in the earth. We do not realize that we are living in its hollows, but assume that we are living on the earth's surface. Imagine someone living in the depths of the sea. He might think that he was living on the surface, and seeing the sun and the other heavenly bodies through the water, he might think that the sea was the sky. He might be so sluggish and feeble that he had never reached the top of the sea, never emerged and raised his head from the sea into this world of ours, and seen for himself – or even heard from someone who had seen it – how much purer and more beautiful it really is than the one in which his people lives. Now we are in just the same position. Although we live in a hollow of the earth, we assume that we are living on the surface, and we call the air heaven, as though it were the heaven through which the stars move. And this point too is the same, that we are too feeble and sluggish to make our way out to the upper limit of the air. If

someone could reach to the summit, or put on wings and
fly aloft, when he put up his head he would see the world
above, just as fishes see our world when they put up their
heads out of the sea; and if his nature were able to bear
the sight, he would recognize that that is the true heaven
and the true light and the true earth. For this earth and
its stones and all the regions in which we live are marred
and corroded, just as in the sea everything is corroded by
the brine, and there is no vegetation worth mentioning,
and scarcely any degree of perfect formation, but only
caverns and sand and measureless mud, and tracts of
slime wherever there is earth as well; and nothing is in
the least worthy to be judged beautiful by our standards.
But the things above excel those of our world to a degree
far greater still. If this is the right moment for an imaginative description, Simmias, it will be worth your while
to hear what it is really like upon the earth which lies
beneath the heavens.'

'Yes, indeed, Socrates,' said Simmias, 'it would be a
great pleasure to us, at any rate, to hear this description.'

'Well, my dear boy,' said Socrates, 'the real earth,
viewed from above, is supposed to look like one of these
balls made of twelve pieces of skin,[54] variegated and
marked out in different colours, of which the colours
which we know are only limited samples, like the paints
which artists use; but there the whole earth is made up
of such colours, and others far brighter and purer still.
One section is a marvellously beautiful purple, and another is golden; all that is white of it is whiter than chalk
or snow; and the rest is similarly made up of the other
colours, still more and lovelier than those which we have
seen. Even these very hollows in the earth, full of water
and air, assume a kind of colour as they gleam amid the
different hues around them, so that there appears to be
one continuous surface of varied colours. The trees and
flowers and fruits which grow upon this earth are pro-

portionately beautiful. The mountains too and the stones have a proportionate smoothness and transparency, and their colours are lovelier. The pebbles which are so highly prized in our world – the jaspers and rubies and emeralds and the rest – are fragments of these stones; but there everything is as beautiful as they are, or better still. This is because the stones there are in their natural state, not damaged by decay and corroded by salt water as ours are by the sediment which has collected here, and which causes disfigurement and disease to stones and earth, and animals and plants as well. The earth itself is adorned not only with all these stones but also with gold and silver and the other metals, for many rich veins of them occur in plain view in all parts of the earth, so that to see them is a sight for the eyes of the blessed.

'There are many kinds of animals upon it, and also human beings, some of whom live inland, others round the air, as we live round the sea, and others in islands surrounded by air but close to the mainland. In a word, as water and the sea are to us for our purposes, so is air to them; and as air is to us, so the ether is to them. Their climate is so temperate that they are free from disease and live much longer than people do here; and in sight and hearing and understanding and all other faculties they are as far superior to us as air is to water or ether to air in clarity.

'They also have sanctuaries and temples which are truly inhabited by gods; and oracles and prophecies and visions and all other kinds of communion with the gods occur there face to face. They see the sun and moon and stars as they really are; and the rest of their happiness is after the same manner.

'Such is the nature of the earth as a whole and of the things that are upon it. In the earth itself, all over its surface, there are many hollow regions, some deeper and more widely spread than that in which we live, others deeper than our region but with a smaller expanse, some both shallower than ours and broader. All these are joined together underground by many connecting channels, some narrower, some wider, through which, from one basin to another, there flows a great volume of water, monstrous unceasing subterranean rivers of waters both hot and cold; and of fire too, great rivers of fire; and many of liquid mud, some clearer, some more turbid, like the rivers in Sicily that flow mud before the lava comes, and the lava-stream itself. By these the several regions are filled in turn as the flood reaches them.

'All this movement to and fro is caused by an oscillation inside the earth, and this oscillation is brought about by natural means, as follows.

'One of the cavities in the earth is not only larger than the rest, but pierces right through from one side to the other. It is of this that Homer speaks when he says [55]

Far, far away, where lies earth's deepest chasm;

while elsewhere both he and many other poets refer to it as Tartarus. Into this gulf all the rivers flow together, and from it they flow forth again; and each acquires the nature of that part of the earth through which it flows. The cause of the flowing in and out of all these streams is that the mass of liquid has no bottom or foundation; so it oscillates and surges to and fro, and the air or breath [56] that belongs to it does the same; for it accompanies the liquid both as it rushes to the further side of the earth and as it returns to this. And just as when we breathe we exhale and inhale the breath in a continuous stream, so in this case too the breath, oscillating with the liquid, causes terrible and monstrous winds as it passes in and out. So when the water retires to the so-called [57] lower region the streams in the earth flow into those parts and irrigate them fully; and when in turn it ebbs from there and rushes back this way, it fills our streams again, and when they are filled they flow through their channels and through the earth; and arriving in those

175

regions to which their ways have been severally prepared,
they make seas and lakes and rivers and springs. Then
sinking again beneath the ground, some by way of more
and further regions, others by fewer and nearer, they
empty themselves once more into Tartarus, some much
lower, some only a little lower than the point at which
they were emitted; but they all flow in at a level deeper
than their rise. Some flow in on the opposite side [58] to
that on which they came out, and others on the same side;
while some make a complete circle and, winding like a
snake one or even more times round the earth, [59] descend
as far as possible before they again discharge their waters.
It is possible to descend in either direction as far as the
centre, but no further; for either direction from the
centre is uphill, whichever way the streams are flowing.

'Among these many various mighty streams there are
four in particular. The greatest of these, and the one
which describes the outermost circle, is that which is
called Oceanus. Directly opposite to this and with a
contrary course is Acheron, which not only flows
through other desolate regions but passes underground
and arrives at the Acherusian Lake; where the souls of
the dead for the most part come, and after staying there
for certain fixed periods, longer or shorter, are sent forth
again to the births of living creatures. Half way between
these two a third river has its rise, and near its source
issues into a great place burning with sheets of fire, where
it forms a boiling lake of muddy water greater than our
sea. From there it follows a circular course, flowing turbid and muddy; and as it winds round inside the earth
it comes at last to the margin of the Acherusian Lake,
but does not mingle with the waters; and after many
windings under ground, it plunges into Tartarus at a
lower point. This is the river called Pyriphlegethon,
whose fiery stream belches forth jets of lava here and
there in all parts of the world. Directly opposite to this

in its turn the fourth river breaks out, first, they say, into a wild and dreadful place, all leaden grey, [60] which is called the Stygian region, and the lake which the river forms on its entry is called Styx. After falling into this, and acquiring mysterious powers in its waters, the river passes underground and follows a spiral course contrary to that of Pyriphlegethon, which it meets from the opposite direction in the Acherusian Lake. This river too mingles its stream with no other waters, but circling round falls into Tartarus opposite Pyriphlegethon; and its name, the poets say, is Cocytus.

'Such is the conformation of the earth and its rivers. And when the newly dead reach the place to which each is conducted by his guardian spirit, first they submit to judgement; both those who have lived well and holily, and those who have not. Those who are judged to have lived a neutral life set out for Acheron, and embarking in those vessels which await them, are conveyed in them to the lake; and there they dwell, and undergoing purification are both absolved by punishment from any sins that they have committed, and rewarded for their good deeds, according to each man's deserts. Those who on account of the greatness of their sins are judged to be incurable, as having committed many gross acts of sacrilege or many wicked and lawless murders or any other such crimes – these are hurled by their appropriate destiny into Tartarus, from whence they emerge no more.

'Others are judged to have been guilty of sins which, though great, are curable; if, for example, they have offered violence to father or mother in a fit of passion, but spent the rest of their lives in penitence, or if they have committed manslaughter after the same fashion. These too must be cast into Tartarus; but when this has been done and they have remained there for a year, the surge casts them out – the manslayers down Cocytus and the offenders against their parents down Pyriphlegethon. And when, as they are swept along, they come past the

Acherusian Lake, there they cry aloud and call upon those whom they have killed or misused, and calling, beg and entreat for leave to pass from the stream into the lake, and be received by them. If they prevail, they come out and there is an end of their distress; but if not, they are swept away once more into Tartarus and from there back into the rivers, and find no release from their sufferings until they prevail upon those whom they have wronged; for this is the punishment which their judge has appointed for them.

'But those who are judged to have lived a life of surpassing holiness – these are they who are released and set free from confinement in these regions of the earth, and passing upward to their pure abode, make their dwelling upon the earth's surface. And of these such as have purified themselves sufficiently by philosophy live thereafter altogether without bodies, and reach habitations even more beautiful, which it is not easy to portray – nor is there time to do so now. But the reasons which we have already described provide ground enough, as you can see, Simmias, for leaving nothing undone to attain during life some measure of goodness and wisdom; for the prize is glorious and the hope great.

'Of course, no reasonable man ought to insist that the facts are exactly as I have described them. But that either this or something very like it is a true account of our souls and their future habitations – since we have clear evidence that the soul is immortal – this, I think, is both a reasonable contention and a belief worth risking; for the risk is a noble one. We should use such accounts to inspire ourselves with confidence; and that is why I have already drawn out my tale so long.

'There is one way, then, in which a man can be free from all anxiety about the fate of his soul; if in life he has abandoned bodily pleasures and adornments, as foreign to his purpose and likely to do more harm than good, and has devoted himself to the pleasures of acquiring knowledge; and so by decking his soul not with a borrowed beauty but with its own – with self-control, and goodness, and courage, and liberality, and truth – has fitted himself to await his journey to the next world. You, Simmias and Cebes and the rest, will each make this journey some day in the future; but "for me the fated hour" (as a tragic character might say) "calls even now". In other words, it is about time that I took my bath. I prefer to have a bath before drinking the poison, rather than give the women the trouble of washing me when I am dead.'

When he had finished speaking, Crito said 'Very well, Socrates. But have you no directions for the others or myself about your children or anything else? What can we do to please you best?'

'Nothing new, Crito,' said Socrates; 'just what I am always telling you. If you look after yourselves, whatever you do will please me and mine and you too, even if you don't agree with me now. On the other hand, if you neglect yourselves and fail to follow the line of life as I have laid it down both now and in the past, however fervently you agree with me now, it will do no good at all.'

'We shall try our best to do as you say,' said Crito. 'But how shall we bury you?'

'Any way you like,' replied Socrates, 'that is, if you can catch me and I don't slip through your fingers.' He laughed gently as he spoke, and turning to us went on: 'I can't persuade Crito that I am this Socrates here who is talking to you now and marshalling all the arguments; he thinks that I am the one whom he will see presently lying dead; and he asks how he is to bury me! As for my long and elaborate explanation that when I have drunk the poison I shall remain with you no longer, but depart to a state of heavenly happiness, this attempt to console both you and myself seems to be wasted on him. You must give an assurance to Crito for me – the oppo-

site of the one which he gave to the court which tried me.
He undertook that I should stay; but you must assure
him that when I am dead I shall not stay, but depart and
be gone. That will help Crito to bear it more easily, and
keep him from being distressed on my account when he
sees my body being burned or buried, as if something
dreadful were happening to me; or from saying at the
funeral that it is Socrates whom he is laying out or
carrying to the grave or burying. Believe me, my dear
friend Crito: mis-statements are not merely jarring in
their immediate context; they also have a bad effect upon
the soul. No, you must keep up your spirits and say that
it is only my body that you are burying; and you can
bury it as you please, in whatever way you think is most
proper.'

With these words he got up and went into another
room to bathe; and Crito went after him, but told us to
wait. So we waited, discussing and reviewing what had
been said, or else dwelling upon the greatness of the
calamity which had befallen us; for we felt just as though
we were losing a father and should be orphans for the
rest of our lives. Meanwhile, when Socrates had taken
his bath, his children were brought to see him – he had
two little sons and one big boy – and the women of his
household – you know – arrived. He talked to them in
Crito's presence and gave them directions about carrying
out his wishes; then he told the women and children to
go away, and came back himself to join us.

It was now nearly sunset, because he had spent a long
time inside. He came and sat down, fresh from the bath;
and he had only been talking for a few minutes when the
prison officer came in, and walked up to him. 'Socrates,'
he said, 'at any rate I shall not have to find fault with you,
as I do with others, for getting angry with me and
cursing when I tell them to drink the poison – carrying
out Government orders. I have come to know during
this time that you are the noblest and the gentlest and the

bravest of all the men that have ever come here, and now especially I am sure that you are not angry with me, but with them; because you know who are responsible. So now – you know what I have come to say – goodbye, and try to bear what must be as easily as you can.' As he spoke he burst into tears, and turning round, went away.

Socrates looked up at him and said 'Goodbye to you, too; we will do as you say.' Then addressing us he went on 'What a charming person! All the time I have been here he has visited me, and sometimes had discussions with me, and shown me the greatest kindness; and how generous of him now to shed tears for me at parting! But come, Crito, let us do as he says. Someone had better bring in the poison, if it is ready prepared; if not, tell the man to prepare it.'

'But surely, Socrates,' said Crito, 'the sun is still upon the mountains; it has not gone down yet. Besides, I know that in other cases people have dinner and enjoy their wine, and sometimes the company of those whom they love, long after they receive the warning; and only drink the poison quite late at night. No need to hurry; there is still plenty of time.'

'It is natural that these people whom you speak of should act in that way, Crito,' said Socrates, 'because they think that they gain by it. And it is also natural that I should not; because I believe that I should gain nothing by drinking the poison a little later – I should only make myself ridiculous in my own eyes if I clung to life and hugged it when it has no more to offer. Come, do as I say and don't make difficulties.'

At this Crito made a sign to his servant, who was standing near by. The servant went out and after spending a considerable time returned with the man who was to administer the poison; he was carrying it ready prepared in a cup. When Socrates saw him he said 'Well, my good fellow, you understand these things; what ought I to do?'

'Just drink it,' he said, 'and then walk about until you feel a weight in your legs, and then lie down. Then it will act of its own accord.'

As he spoke he handed the cup to Socrates, who received it quite cheerfully, Echecrates, without a tremor, without any change of colour or expression, and said, looking up under his brows with his usual steady gaze 'What do you say about pouring a libation from this drink? Is it permitted, or not?'

'We only prepare what we regard as the normal dose, Socrates,' he replied.

'I see,' said Socrates. 'But I suppose I am allowed, or rather bound, to pray the gods that my removal from this world to the other may be prosperous. This is my prayer, then; and I hope that it may be granted.' With these words, quite calmly and with no sign of distaste, he drained the cup in one breath.

Up till this time most of us had been fairly successful in keeping back our tears; but when we saw that he was drinking, that he had actually drunk it, we could do so no longer; in spite of myself the tears came pouring out, so that I covered my face and wept broken-heartedly – not for him, but for my own calamity in losing such a friend. Crito had given up even before me, and had gone out when he could not restrain his tears. But Apollodorus, who had never stopped crying even before, now broke out into such a storm of passionate weeping that he made everyone in the room break down, except Socrates himself, who said:

'Really, my friends, what a way to behave! Why, that was my main reason for sending away the women, to prevent this sort of disturbance; because I am told that one should make one's end in a tranquil frame of mind. Calm yourselves and try to be brave.'

This made us feel ashamed, and we controlled our tears. Socrates walked about, and presently, saying that his legs were heavy, lay down on his back – that was what the man recommended. The man (he was the same one who had administered the poison) kept his hand upon Socrates, and after a little while examined his feet and legs; then pinched his foot hard and asked if he felt it. Socrates said no. Then he did the same to his legs; and moving gradually upwards in this way let us see that he was getting cold and numb. Presently he felt him again and said that when it reached the heart, Socrates would be gone.

The coldness was spreading about as far as his waist when Socrates uncovered his face – for he had covered it up – and said (they were his last words): 'Crito, we ought to offer a cock to Asclepius.[61] See to it, and don't forget.'

'No, it shall be done,' said Crito. 'Are you sure that there is nothing else?'

Socrates made no reply to this question, but after a little while he stirred; and when the man uncovered him, his eyes were fixed. When Crito saw this, he closed the mouth and eyes.

Such, Echecrates, was the end of our comrade, who was, we may fairly say, of all those whom we knew in our time, the bravest and also the wisest and most upright man.

NOTES TO *Euthyphro*

1. *the Lyceum:* The precinct of Apollo Lyceius, on the north-east side of Athens; it included a recreation ground and some buildings in which Aristotle later set up his philosophical school.

2. *the King Archon* was a magistrate who inherited the priestly functions formerly held by the king, and therefore presided at all religious trials, including prosecutions for homicide, which involved religious pollution.

3. *Meletus:* For details of the accusation brought against Socrates the reader is referred to the *Apology*.

4. *an inventor of gods:* The Greek suggests a metaphor (from issuing counterfeit money) which is difficult to sustain in English. For Socrates' 'supernatural voice' see *Apology* 40 A.

5. *predicting the future:* Apparently as a freelance; he does not seem to have held any official position.

6. *without charging a fee:* Unlike the Sophists; cf. *Apology* 19 E.

7. *a nimble opponent:* Literally 'a flier'. There is a joke here; in Greek the same word means *prosecute* and *pursue;* and 'to pursue birds flying' was a proverbial expression for a crazy undertaking.

8. *pollution of his guilt:* Euthyphro's prosecution of his father is very likely a dramatic fiction, introduced by Plato to exemplify an extreme clash of 'pieties', and in particular to lead up to Euthyphro's argument from traditional mythology (5E) and the theological difficulties that follow from it. Socrates' attitude is rather surprising, and it is clearly inconsistent with his doctrine (*Gorgias* 480 B) that wrongdoers must be brought to justice in their own interest; perhaps his remark is simply designed to draw Euthyphro out. Certainly Euthyphro seems more enlightened – until it appears that his motives are partly dictated by self-interest. The fact is that the whole dialogue is exploratory and provocative; a great many points are raised, and the reader is left to decide them for himself in the light of the many half-truths and suggestions contributed by both parties.

9. *Naxos* is the largest of the Cyclades, a group of islands in the west central Aegean. Since Athens lost control of it in 404 B.C. (five years before the dramatic date of the dialogue),

some critics have seen a chronological difficulty here; but (as noted above) the whole story is probably fictitious.

10. *proper authority:* 'The Interpreter', an official adviser on matters of religion, especially ceremonial purification.

11. *characteristic:* The Greek word is that from which we get our 'idea', and Socrates' language is no doubt intended to point forward to Plato's Theory of Forms or Ideas (Introduction, p. 14).

12. *not to prosecute . . . is impious:* Euthyphro's first attempted definition exhibits the common fault of adducing a particular (or quasi-particular) instance of the definiendum.

13. *on similar grounds:* These curiously primitive stories are found in Hesiod, *Theogony* 126 ff., 453 ff. Uranus (Heaven) did not swallow his children, the Titans, but imprisoned them deep in the body of his consort Gaia (Earth); she encouraged them to assert themselves, and Cronos, the youngest but most formidable of them, attacked Uranus and castrated him. To avoid such a fate for himself, he swallowed his own children as they were born; but his wife Rhea smuggled the infant Zeus away to Crete and put his baby-clothes on a stone, which Cronos swallowed; it acted as an emetic and made him vomit up the other children. Zeus later led a revolt against him and put him in chains.

14. *must assent too:* This is clearly sarcastic. In point of fact the cruder stories about the gods had been ridiculed or at least rejected by many thinkers and poets (including Xenophanes, Pindar, Aeschylus and Euripides); and probably few people took them seriously at this date – except as evidence in support of their own arguments.

15. *poets:* E.g., Homer in the *Iliad,* where the gods are violently divided for and against the Greeks.

16. *the great Panathenaic festival* was held every four years. The robe was an offering to Athene, and was carried in a splendid procession, which is represented on the frieze of the Parthenon.

17. *pattern:* Another step towards the theory of Forms, which Plato often describes (in the earlier dialogues) as patterns. Note, however, that there is absolutely no ground for assuming that his use of this metaphor in a work intended for the general public reflects the latest development of his own thought at the time of writing.

18. *the form that I wanted:* This second definition is at least general, and supplies a basis for discussion.

19. *god-beloved:* This and *god-hated* are awkward terms, but they are almost indispensable if the course of the argument is to be reproduced concisely.

20. *Hera* was the mother of Hephaestus, and threw him down from Olympus because he was deformed; in revenge he sent her a magic chair which held her fast when she sat in it. Hence (although they were later reconciled) they furnish another example of hostility between parent and child.

21. *because it is loved:* This question has much exercised both philosophers and theologians. Plato undoubtedly held the first alternative to be true, since for him moral values were absolute. Here he discredits the second by involving Euthyphro in a contradiction; but in any case 'what is loved by the gods' could only give the genus of piety, not its definition; for presumably they also love other kinds of goodness.

22. *different:* They describe respectively *patient* and *agent*, *effect* and *cause*.

23. *produced:* The relation of product to producer is not relevant here; it is included simply for completeness.

24. *essence . . . attributes:* Apparently the first appearance of this important logical distinction, and the first indication that the definition of anything must describe the essence of that thing, i.e., the quality or qualities without which it would no longer be itself. Strictly speaking, *attributes* may be either essential or non-essential (accidents); here the word is used in the latter sense.

25. *Daedalus* was by tradition the inventive master of many arts, including sculpture; the story that he made his figures move is attributed to the innovation of separating the feet of a statue. By claiming him as an ancestor Socrates only means that his father was a sculptor.

26. *Tantalus* was the son of an earth-goddess of Wealth; and it was his remarkable prosperity that bred the reckless arrogance by which he earned his famous punishment.

27. *demoralized:* Socrates means (as he makes clearer below) that the luxury of expert knowledge has made Euthyphro lazy in argument. After the interlude Socrates makes a fresh start

by suggesting that piety is a species of the genus 'moral rectitude'. (The distinction of genus and species is here clearly made for the first time, by the illustration of fear and reverence.) Plato is preparing for the process of definition by 'division' which he uses in the *Sophist* and *Politicus*.

28. *younger:* And therefore should be more agile (intellectually).

29. *the poet:* Who he was is unknown.

30. *what kind:* Here is at least the germ of Aristotle's doctrine that definition is of species, and that a species is defined by the *genus* which includes it and the *differentia* which distinguishes it from all other species of that genus.

31. *scalene . . . isosceles:* These terms do not seem to be used elsewhere of numbers, but they are clearly intended to describe numbers which respectively are and are not divisible into two equal integers.

32. *tendance:* A convenient (if unfamiliar) word to cover the meanings of *service to* and *care of* – the latter is presently rejected. Piety is now defined as one species of moral rectitude.

33. *slaves:* 'Apprentices' would convey the meaning better, since (as the following examples show) the kind of service intended is help in the performance of professional duties.

34. *ruins everything:* Euthyphro has probably never considered what the grand purpose is for which man's co-operation is required, and falls back upon the orthodox attitude of the State religion.

35. *all the information that I wanted:* This is surely a broad hint that the right answer to Socrates' question would yield a satisfactory definition. If Plato had supplied the answer it would probably have been 'the just and orderly government of the world'; but no doubt he wanted his readers to think this out for themselves.

36. *the lover . . . his love:* Socrates is a lover of argument.

37. *in a circle:* Daedalus only freed them from immobility (11 c).

38. *at an earlier stage:* 10 D–11 A.

39. *Proteus* was an omniscient sea-deity who tried to elude his questioners by changing into all kinds of shapes, but yielded at last if they held on tenaciously (Homer, *Odyssey* IV. 382 ff., Virgil, *Georgics* IV. 437 ff.).

40. *think you know:* Note the qualification; Socrates no longer asserts that Euthyphro *does* know. In fact he has done his best to point out and to shatter Euthyphro's misplaced self-

confidence, and so to prepare him for the attainment of true wisdom. But Euthyphro (though he keeps his temper) feels that he has had enough.

41. *the rest of my life:* Socrates' protest is only mock-serious; but there is a touch of dramatic irony in the last few words, because his life is now very near its end.

1. *in the open spaces of this city:* Literally 'at the bankers' counters in the market-place'; but this sounds odd in English, and conveys the false impression that he had business there; it was simply a good place for meeting people.

2. *Anytus and his colleagues:* viz. Meletus and Lycon. Meletus, a fiery and unpleasant young man, who probably had a personal grudge against Socrates, was the leader of the prosecution; Anytus, an honest and influential democrat who hated the Sophists and perhaps regarded Socrates as one of them, gave it weight and an air of respectability; Lycon was a rhetorician and contributed eloquence.

3. *a playwright:* The comic poet Aristophanes burlesqued Socrates in his comedy the *Clouds*, produced in 423, by representing him as a Sophist of the worst type – a quack scientist and rhetorician with neither religion nor morals. No doubt he chose Socrates simply as a perfect subject for caricature, and meant him no harm (the two men are quite friendly in the *Symposium*); but the play probably had a damaging effect.

4. *Socrates goes whirling round:* He appears suspended in a basket, because his mind works better in the upper air.

5. *Gorgias of Leontini* was a sceptic and a brilliant rhetorician who first visited Athens on a diplomatic mission in 427 and later settled there for some time. In the dialogue called after him Plato represents him as a well-meaning simple-minded elderly don who is no match for Socrates.

6. *Prodicus of Ceos* specialized in the study of synonyms and distinctions of meaning; his style is parodied in the *Protagoras*. He was a distinguished teacher and one of the best of the Sophists in spite of his pedantry.

7. *Hippias of Elis* was supposed to know something about everything, including the useful arts. It is unlikely that his knowledge was profound.

8. *Callias* is the host in the *Protagoras*. He was a great patron of sophists, and ruined himself by this and other expensive habits.

9. *Evenus of Paros* was a rhetorician and poet (mentioned also in the *Phaedo*, p. 102) who was staying at this time in Athens.

'Twenty guineas' is a rough but reasonable equivalent for 'five minae'. Mr G. B. Kerford, in a generous review, has pointed out that my English money equivalents (based on the nominal silver value of the drachma) should be multiplied by about 15 to fit present conditions. On this principle Evenus' fee (p. 48) would be 300 guineas; Anaxagoras' book (p. 57) would cost 15s.; Socrates' self-proposed fine (p. 72) would be £75; and so on.

10. *Delphi:* The oracle of Apollo at Delphi was the supreme authority whose advice was sought on all kinds of subjects – religious, moral, political, and personal. The source of its information remains a mystery; if it relied upon a secret service, the secret was efficiently kept. The only 'natural' explanation of its reply about Socrates is that it was well aware of his true character and ideals and thoroughly approved of them.

11. *Chaerephon:* Little can be added to the account given here, except that he was one of the few democrats in Socrates' circle, and that he too appeared in the *Clouds*.

12. *the recent expulsion,* etc., refers to the events of 404, when the oligarchs, seizing power, murdered or drove out large numbers of their political opponents; these, under the leadership of Thrasybulus, presently gained a footing in Attica, defeated the oligarchs, and restored the democracy in the following year.

13. *his brother:* Chaerecrates.

14. *Dog!:* Such pseudo-oaths were not peculiar to Socrates, nor did he always avoid the name of a real deity. The practice was perhaps originally pious, but by this date had become humorous.

15. *pilgrimage* seems a legitimate equivalent for the literal 'labours' (e.g. of Hercules), though the latter were mainly for the benefit of mankind.

16. *Council ... Assembly:* The Council (of 500 members) was the supreme administrative authority; the Assembly was open to all adult male citizens.

17. *sun and moon are gods:* The cult of the sun was prevalent in Greece, though it tended to be merged in the worship of Apollo. The moon (associated with Artemis and Hecate) was of especial importance in magic. The object of the question is to lead up to the doctrines of Anaxagoras.

18. *Anaxagoras of Clazomenae* (about 500–428), one of the most original thinkers of the century, resided in Athens for thirty years. In 450 he was accused of impiety and collaboration with Persia, and condemned to death (?), but escaped with the help of Pericles, who was his very good friend, and retired to Lampsacus, where he died. The details of the story are disputed, but there is little doubt that the motives underlying his accusation were not religious or patriotic but political, and formed part of a campaign against Pericles and his advisers. Clearly Plato intends us to compare the circumstances of the two trials and to contrast their consequences. The only features of Anaxagoras' teaching that concern us are his astronomical views (that the sun and moon are fragments of the earth which have become white-hot by the rapidity of their movement) and his doctrine of Mind (referred to in the *Phaedo*, p. 155).

19. *in the market-place:* Plato says 'in the orchestra', that is, the flat circular space (in which the chorus dances) in front of the stage in the open-air Theatre. It would have been both vacant and accessible on most days of the year, and was therefore quite a suitable place for bookstalls.

20. *supernatural beings:* 'daemons'. The word has a vague connotation, but is generally used of any being or agency that is more than human but not quite identifiably divine. The corresponding adjective often simply means 'mysterious'. It is used here with reference to Socrates' 'warning voice'.

21. *bastard children:* the heroes and demigods of mythology.

22. *son of Thetis:* Achilles. The passage which Socrates partly paraphrases and partly quotes is *Iliad* xviii. 94–106.

23. *Potidaea* in Chalcidice revolted from Athens in 432 and was reduced two years later. In the preliminary fighting Socrates saved the life of Alcibiades, as the latter relates in the *Symposium* (220 D).

24. *Amphipolis:* An Athenian colony at the mouth of the Strymon (Struma). The battle to which Socrates refers took place outside the walls in 422.

25. *Delium* in Boeotia was the scene of a heavy Athenian defeat in 424. According to Alcibiades in the passage quoted above, Socrates showed great gallantry.

26. *elected to the Council:* Appointment was actually by lot; but this and other technical details unimportant to the general

sense (and in some cases tedious to explain) have been glossed over in the translation of this paragraph.

27. *the naval engagement:* The Athenian victory at Arginusae in 406. Public feeling ran very high at this negligence of the admirals (or generals – land and sea commands were not distinguished at Athens). Only eight were in fact implicated, two being absent from the battle.

28. *Round Chamber:* A building used as a Government office, normally by the executive of the Council.

29. *dreams:* e.g. the one described in the *Phaedo*, p. 103.

30. *Crito:* Socrates' closest friend, who gives his name to the next dialogue. The other persons mentioned are either unknown or unimportant, except Plato himself, his father Ariston, his brother Adimantus (who figures largely in the *Republic*) and Apollodorus, the narrator of the *Symposium*, whose excitability makes him rather a nuisance in the *Phaedo*.

31. *Sphettus* and *Cephisia* were 'demes' or parishes in Attica.

32. *from a tree or from a rock:* Odyssey xix. 163. This proverbial expression, implying 'so you must have *some* parents' is used by Penelope in encouraging the disguised Odysseus to reveal his name and family.

33. *sons:* Lamprocles, Sophroniscus, and Menexenus. Unfortunately they did not take after their father.

34. *thirty votes:* Apparently 220 voted for and 280 against acquittal; but 30 is probably a round number.

35. *one-fifth of the votes:* Socrates pretends that each of the accusers has obtained one-third of the votes cast for the prosecution, so that Meletus has only 93 odd instead of 100. He must have enjoyed this brazen illogicality. The fine was 1,000 drachmae.

36. *free maintenance:* This was actually provided for distinguished citizens and public benefactors in the Prytaneum, a sort of State hotel.

37. *banishment:* No doubt this was exactly what most of his enemies desired.

38. *five pounds:* 'One mina'. According to Xenophon *Oeconomica* ii. 3, this would have been one-fifth of Socrates' entire resources. (See also note 9, pp. 190–1.)

39. *those who voted for my execution:* Apparently 80 more than had voted for his condemnation, so that 360 favoured death and only 140 the fine.

40. *as we are told:* The doctrines of the soul's immortality and rebirth, and of purification by punishment in the underworld belong to Orphism, a primitive but in some ways remarkably enlightened religion which perhaps came to Greece from Thrace and certainly inspired the 'mystery cults' which were practised in various parts of Greece, especially at Eleusis in Attica. These were liable to abuse and were conventionally regarded with some disdain, but they were a valuable supplement to the formalities of official religion. Orphism was largely adopted by the Pythagoreans, who had a great influence upon Socrates and Plato.

41. *the Great King:* The king of Persia, regarded as a type of worldly prosperity.

42. *Minos, Rhadamanthys, and Aeacus* were by tradition mortal sons of Zeus, and became judges in the underworld as a reward for their earthly justice and piety.

43. *Triptolemus* was the introducer of agriculture and had an important part in the cult of Demeter at the Eleusinian Mysteries. He is not described elsewhere as a judge of the dead.

44. *Orpheus* is no doubt mentioned not as a singer and poet but as the founder of Orphism.

45. *Musaeus* was a bard like Orpheus, but his benefactions consisted in giving oracles and instruction for the curing of disease.

46. *Hesiod* of Ascra in Boeotia was the first didactic poet; he was generally ranked next after Homer in antiquity and merit.

47. *Palamedes*, a Greek warrior in the Trojan War, exposed a discreditable trick on the part of Odysseus, who by forged evidence got him executed for treason (Virgil, *Aeneid* ii. 81ff).

48. *Ajax* expected to be awarded the arms of Achilles, which were supposed to pass, after their owner's death, to the next bravest of the Greeks; but the generals Agamemnon and Menelaus awarded them to Odysseus. Ajax, in a fit of madness, killed some cattle in mistake for the persons who had wronged him, and later, recovering his senses, was so ashamed that he killed himself.

49. *Sisyphus* was a king of Corinth who was famous for his unscrupulous cleverness. Presumably it was his brains rather than his character that interested Socrates.

NOTES TO *Crito*

1. *Sunium:* A headland at the southern extremity of Attica and about thirty miles from Athens.

2. *To the pleasant land,* etc.: The line is an echo of *Iliad* ix. 363, where Phthia (in eastern Thessaly) is the homeland of Achilles; and probably the suggestion here is simply that Socrates is going home.

3. *Simmias* and *Cebes* conduct most of the discussion with Socrates in the *Phaedo*.

4. *when it was quite unnecessary:* Socrates might have left the country before the trial came on.

5. *Sparta or Crete:* Socrates admired these states because of their respect for law and order. The fact that they were oligarchies gave his opponents another political handle.

6. *Thebes* and *Megara* adjoined Attica on the north-west and south-west respectively. They too were oligarchies; the Laws are being a trifle sarcastic.

7. *an enemy to their constitution:* Not as being a democrat, but as a law-breaker.

8. *roystering in Thessaly:* The phrase is semi-proverbial; the Thessalian 'barons' were notorious for their luxury. The constant repetition of the name 'Thessaly' is intended to be scornful.

9. *a mystic:* The actual reference is to worshippers of the Asiatic goddess Cybele, whose rites were accompanied by exciting music. The point seems to be that in devout ears the music goes on ringing when the playing has ceased. But the main object of the simile, with its religious associations, is no doubt to suggest that the voice of the Laws is only another expression of the 'inner voice' which (as the last line of the dialogue makes clear) is the voice of God.

1. *hemlock:* Poisoning by means of hemlock-juice (conium) seems to have been a common method of execution at Athens. Death was apparently painless but rather slow.
2. *Apollodorus* has already been mentioned in *The Apology*.
3. *Critobulus* was the son of Crito.
4. *Simmias* and *Cebes* were disciples of Philolaus the Pythagorean. Like Phaedo, they were quite young men. After Socrates himself, they are the chief characters of the 'inner' dialogue. Simmias is quick-witted and inclined to be hasty; Cebes is accurate, critical, and difficult to convince.
5. *Xanthippe:* There is nothing in Plato's account to suggest that she was a shrew, although there are two outspoken comments on her in Xenophon, and many unkind anecdotes in later writers. She should not be judged too harshly; Socrates must have been a most trying husband.
6. *the allegory:* This is an Orphic doctrine.
7. *as we have been told:* This too is Orphic.
8. *our fellow-countrymen:* The Boeotians were dull people and had no use for intellectuals.
9. *absolute uprightness:* Or 'moral goodness', or 'justice'. Here the Forms appear for the first time, but so far merely as Absolutes which can only be apprehended by the mind.
10. *a comic poet:* Probably though not necessarily Aristophanes.
11. *an old legend:* The Orphic doctrine of transmigration.
12. *come into being:* The argument which follows is slightly obscured by the fact that Greek uses one word (not unreasonably) to cover the senses of *birth, generation, coming from,* and *coming to be* or *into being.* The last is often the most convenient English equivalent, but it never implies 'out of nothing'; it is always a process from one state to another. Thus if souls are reborn they must be reborn out of some kind of existence.
13. *Endymion* was loved by the Moon-goddess and (granted immortality) sleeps everlastingly.
14. *all things together:* The state of complete mixture and confusion which is reduced to order by Mind.
15. *a diagram:* So in the *Meno* a boy slave, by the aid of a diagram

and a series of questions from Socrates, solves a geometrical problem without any knowledge of geometry.

16. *equality:* The Forms are introduced again; this time as eternal changeless patterns which the soul must have known before birth, because it is reminded of them by imperfect copies, and could never have apprehended them through the senses.

17. *Hades:* This word has generally been banished from the translation, because to many it is a facetious synonym for Hell. Here Plato stresses its etymology and proper meaning.

18. *Penelope* was besieged by suitors during the absence of her husband Odysseus. She told them that she would make up her mind when she had finished her weaving; and then unwove her day's work every night.

19. *cut off . . . hair* as a sign of mourning.

20. *the Argives* cut off their hair in grief for a part of their territory which they ceded to Sparta after a heavy defeat.

21. *Iolaus* was the 'squire' of Heracles, and helped him effectively when attacked simultaneously by the Hydra and a huge crab.

22. *standard of reality:* In other words with the Theory of Forms.

23. *in the Odyssey:* xx. 17 f.

24. *Harmonia:* A piece of whimsicality. The theory of attunement or harmony, coming as it does from a Theban, suggests the name of Harmonia the wife of Cadmus, king of Thebes. The second objection is therefore identified with Cadmus.

25. *when I was young:* Most of this autobiography is no doubt strictly true. The first theory was held by Socrates' teacher friend Archelaus; the views about the seat of intelligence are attributable as follows: *blood* to Empedocles, *air* to Diogenes of Apollonia, *fire* to Heraclitus, *brain* and the 'ladder of consciousness' to Alcmaeon of Croton.

26. *cause of growth:* This illustration is partly designed to lead up to the problems which follow, but it also suggests, at the very outset of the inquiry into causation, a vital distinction. Nourishment is only a necessary physical condition of growth; a *sine qua non*, not a cause; it does not even supply the *how*, much less the *why*.

27. *by a head:* Another source of confusion is indicated (it is discussed more fully later, p. 159). In Greek, as in English, *measure of difference or degree* is expressed by the same formula

as *agency*. 'By' in 'taller by a head' does not mean the same as 'by' in 'killed by robbers'.

28. *by the addition:* Another distinction: this time 'by' expresses the *manner* or *method* of obtaining a result. The examples themselves are unimportant, although such problems did exercise the minds of fifth-century thinkers.

29. *pleased me:* Socrates speaks as if Anaxagoras first put the idea into his head. It seems more likely that his rational and moral outlook (which was probably congenital) always made him seek for a teleological explanation; and that it was this that made him dissatisfied with materialistic theories.

30. *flat or round:* The view that the earth is spherical is ascribed to Pythagoras.

31. *in the centre:* This was the common belief, though fourth-century Pythagoreans taught that the earth (like the sun, moon, and planets) revolved round a 'central fire', and in the third century Aristarchus of Samos put forward a helio-centric theory.

32. *orbits:* The Greek word really refers to the apparent move-ment of the sun between the Tropics of Cancer and Capri-corn.

33. *vortex . . . pedestal of air:* These were the views of Empedocles and Anaximenes respectively.

34. *those principles:* At first sight it seems meaningless to assert that the cause of beauty in things is Beauty; but it is a fact that we cannot understand what it is that makes any par-ticular object beautiful until, by comparing it with other beautiful objects, we discover what beauty means. We have to build up a theory by inductive 'trial and error', finding first particular hypotheses which account for particular groups of phenomena, and then more general hypotheses which account for the particular ones. This is the method of Plato's Dialectic as described in the *Republic*; and it is very unlikely to have been developed by Socrates, although his 'adduction' formed the basis of it.

35. *by a head:* In this and the following paragraphs Socrates deals with the misconceptions mentioned on pp. 154–5.

36. *destructive critics:* Who are meant is uncertain, but such 'spoiling tactics' were common among the Sophists and in some quasi-philosophical schools. Plato's point is that criti-cism must be kept to one 'level' at a time.

37. *tallness and shortness:* In leading up to the doctrine that opposite attributes cannot co-exist in the same subject, Plato disposes of an apparent exception. It looks as though Simmias were both tall and short. But to say that he is taller than Socrates and shorter than Phaedo only means that his height is measured by two standards of comparison. Tallness and shortness in this example are expressions of relation, not essential attributes of the subject Simmias.

38. *artificial style:* If this is the right meaning, Socrates is probably referring to the constant rhetorical antithesis.

39. *declines:* Throughout the following discussion Forms and qualities are personified by the military metaphor noted in the Introduction – a metaphor springing naturally from the accepted view that opposites or contraries are in perpetual conflict.

40. *as I myself have done:* In the example on p. 161, where Socrates, compared with Simmias, 'becomes' short, though actually remaining unchanged.

41. *this point:* The principle is now extended from opposites themselves to things which possess them as essential attributes. Heat is incompatible not only with cold but also with snow, which is essentially cold.

42. *two and three:* Two is only mentioned as being the first even number and therefore the most 'likely' opposite. The real point is that three is not the opposite of anything.

43. *uneven:* This step is a preparation for the formal argument on p. 167.

44. *in the exact terms:* Instead of the tautological answer which attributes heat in the body to the Form of Heat, we can now give a more specific answer and attribute it to something which implies the Form of Heat. The specimen answers are mere specimens; fire, fever, and unity are not intended to be the only possible answers to convey the right implication – any other odd number, for example, would have served as well as unity or one-ness. On the other hand, in the conversation which follows, Soul is the only possible answer of this kind, since nothing else (except an attribute of Soul such as consciousness) implies life.

45. *immortal:* 'Undying' would exhibit the analogy better by keeping the same negative prefix; but on all other grounds 'immortal' seems preferable.

46. *we are told:* This is Orphism again.

47. *tries:* It is sometimes difficult, as we learn below.

48. *Aeschylus:* The passage is not extant.

49. *ceremonies:* It was customary to sacrifice to Hecate where three roads met.

50. *said before:* p. 132.

51. *someone:* The imaginative description is probably Plato's own creation, though the prevalence in it of analogy and symmetry rather suggests a Pythagorean origin.

52. *Glaucus:* The reference is generally attached to the celebrated sixth-century metal-worker, but it may belong to Glaucus of Rhegium, who wrote an important History of Music and Poetry at about the time of Socrates' death.

53. *Phasis:* The traditional north-east boundary of the civilized world; it flowed into the east side of the Black Sea near Poti.

54. *twelve pieces of skin:* Each in the shape of a regular pentagon. These when sewn together would form a regular dodecahedron, which, properly stuffed (if the leather was pliable enough) would become reasonably spherical. Play-balls were commonly made in this way.

55. *when he says:* Iliad viii. 14. Tartarus is mentioned *ibid.* 481.

56. *air or breath:* Air accompanies the liquid just as (in the view of the Sicilian medical school) the breath of animals passes through the blood-vessels. The earth is like a living organism.

57. *so-called:* Only from the surface to the centre is 'down'; the antipodes are not 'down under', merely opposite.

58. *opposite side:* Of Tartarus.

59. *round the earth:* Not on the surface but under it.

60. *leaden grey:* What colour Plato meant by 'cyanus' is quite uncertain. The word is often assumed to mean lapis lazuli, but this may be blue, green, violet, reddish, or almost colourless. Although the general evidence suggests a dark metallic blue, 'grey' seems more appropriate to the present context.

61. *a cock to Asclepius:* Asclepius was the god of healing. The cock is either a preliminary offering such as sufferers made before sleeping the night in his precincts with the hope of waking up cured, or (more probably) a thank-offering for cure effected. In either case Socrates implies – with a characteristic mixture of humour, paradox, and piety – that death is the cure for life.

*Some other
Penguin Classics
are described on the
following pages*

PLATO

PROTAGORAS AND MENO

Translated by W. K. C. Guthrie

With the possible exception of the *Symposium*, the *Protagoras* is Plato's dramatic masterpiece. In the house of the wealthy Callias, the famous popular teachers and debaters of the great age of Athens meet to cross swords with each other and with Socrates, and each displays, as well as his wisdom, the foibles and weaknesses to which Plato was so keenly alive. The conversation, like that of the *Meno*, turns on whether the art of successful living and good citizenship can be taught; but whereas the *Protagoras* keeps to the level of practical commonsense, the *Meno* leads on into the heart of Plato's philosophy, to the immortality of the soul and the doctrine of learning as the recollection of pre-natal knowledge. But the problems discussed are of interest and value to us to-day, as are the human quirks and failings which Plato picks out to show us. (L 68)

EURIPIDES
ALCESTIS, IPHIGENIA IN TAURUS,
HIPPOLYTUS

Translated by Philip Vellacott

These plays were originally written to be acted first, then
read; to raise dispute as well as tears, to fascinate, to
irritate, to explode, and to inspire. This critical modernity,
concerned primarily with human life, secondarily with art
and philosophy, is the quality which drew the translator
to Euripides, and which first made him want to translate
and produce his plays. His aim here has been to consider
impartially both the actor and the audience, both the
scholar and the layman. In turning from the Biblical or
Tennysonian English which has served many excellent
versions in the past, he has followed other recent trans-
lators, perhaps going further than some; and has tried in
the verse passages (representing lyric metres in the original)
to dispense with words not now current in good prose.
Although Euripides himself constantly used poetic and
archiac diction, it plainly did not offend the ear of his
contemporaries in the way its English counterpart offends
many ears to-day. No fifth-century Athenian had ever
written serious verse in the vocabulary of Thucydides; but
serious and great verse has been written in the vocabulary
of G. M. Trevelyan. (L 3 1)

SOPHOCLES
THE THEBAN PLAYS

Translated by E. F. Watling

'The translator is not only a good scholar but also a sensitive producer and actor, so that theatrical values are much clearer than usual. The dignity of the great orchestra-theatre is maintained, yet the lines will come easily from the lips of a modern and the plays are revealed as containing many unexpected twists of character and even of humour. ... A trilogy eminently playable.' – E. Martin Browne in *Drama*

'Mr Watling's translation of the dialogue into a "much resolved" form of iambic line and the choruses into rhyming verse is extremely successful; its great beauty and extreme speakability far outweigh the few mistakes. Mr Watling has interesting things to say in his introduction about plays themselves, his methods of translation, and the problems of production.' – *Journal of Hellenic Studies*

'Mr Watling is to be congratulated not only on the lucidity and sound scholarship of the translation, but on his success in enabling the reader to grasp the character of these great dramas and the atmosphere in which they were first enacted.' – *Sheffield Telegraph*. (L3)

APOLLONIUS OF RHODES
THE VOYAGE OF ARGO

Translated by E. V. Rieu

In the *Argonautica* of Apollonius of Rhodes, we have the only full account that the Greeks have left us of Jason's voyage in the good ship Argo in quest of the Golden Fleece, a tale which seems to have stood in their estimation second only to the great cycle of legend that centred in the Trojan War. Apollonius's poem is thus unique, and Dr Rieu argues in his lively introduction, and proves in his translation, that far from deserving the cavalier treatment it has often received from our scholars, it is a magnificent work, which Homer himself would not be surprised to find us reading with enjoyment. For Apollonius, writing as he did some 600 years after the great master, succeeded in introducing a new spirit into the epic tradition. In fact, *The Voyage of Argo* is not an epic in the Homeric sense, but a tale of high romance and incredible adventure, to which the poet lends actuality by his deep understanding of human nature, his unerring eye for a dramatic moment, and his quiet sense of humour. The charm and delicacy of his handling of the fatal love of Medea for Jason are unsurpassed in ancient literature. (L 85)

HOMER

THE ODYSSEY

Translated by E. V. Rieu

'Dr Rieu translates actively and sensitively what is arguably the best story in the world into a prose that is lucid and rapid and has sufficient dignity to sustain the narrative. . . . On the whole he catches the directness and simplicity and poise of the original better than any previous translator. . . . The book is more pleasant to read and to handle than many at ten times its price.' – *Listener*

'A new translation in which Homer's words are still winged, though English, and no attempt is made to insist that the prose of translation need be prosaic.' – *Tribune*

'The homespun humour and deft characterization of the humbler characters lose nothing by the racy English of Dr Rieu's rendering. . . . The proof of the pudding lies in the eating, and this one is, beyond question, being eagerly devoured – a fact easily verified by anyone who travels by bus or train, and supported by the enthusiastic testimony of one's own friends.' – *Time and Tide*

'Dr Rieu has achieved a compromise, admirably adapted to commend to the Greekless novel-reader of to-day on this side of the Atlantic this eternally fresh story from the youth of the world.' – *The Times Literary Supplement*. (L I)

LONGUS
DAPHNIS AND CHLOE

Translated by Paul Turner

Nothing is known of Longus except that he lived in the 2nd or 3rd century A.D. and was born probably in Lesbos, but his *Daphnis and Chloe* is the best and most famous of the Greek novels. It is the story of two foundlings who are brought up as shepherds, fall in love, and after some exciting adventures get married and live happily ever after – which is made somewhat easier for them by the discovery that their real parents are very rich. Though it has often been imitated – *The Winter's Tale* is indirectly derived from it – no one has ever equalled the charm of Longus's original version. His graceful style, his gently satiric humour, and his descriptions of country life fully justify the continued popularity of his novel; and there is something surprisingly modern about the psychological insight with which he traces the growth of love in his young hero and heroine. Their perplexed gropings towards 'the right true end of love' (which have at last been translated in full) are described with such delicacy that they they somehow contrive to be funny without being ridiculous, and form one of the most delightful episodes in this little masterpiece of fiction.
(L 59)